CONDITIONING FOR THE HIGH SCHOOL ATHLETE

CONDITIONING FOR THE HIGH SCHOOL ATHLETE

ALLAN M. LEVY, M.D. & ALLAN WEBB

Contemporary Books, Inc.
Chicago

Library of Congress Cataloging in Publication Data

Levy, Allan M.
  Conditioning for the high school athlete.

  Includes index.
   1. Sports—Physiological aspects.   2. Sports—
Accidents and injuries—Prevention.   3. Exercise.
4. Physical fitness.   I. Webb, Allan, joint author.
II. Title.
RC1235.L49   613.7′1   79-50981
ISBN 0-8092-7338-1
ISBN 0-8092-7337-3 pbk.

Photographs by R. J. Mason

Editorial assistance from Harold Rosenthal

Copyright © 1979 by Allan M. Levy and Allan Webb
All rights reserved
Published by Contemporary Books, Inc.
180 North Michigan Avenue, Chicago, Illinois 60601
Manufactured in the United States of America
Library of Congress Catalog Card Number: 79-50981
International Standard Book Number: 0-8092-7338-1 (cloth)
                          0-8092-7337-3 (paper)

Published simultaneously in Canada by
Beaverbooks
953 Dillingham Road
Pickering, Ontario L1W 1Z7
Canada

Contents

Introduction *vii*

1 ... and try not to get hurt *1*

2 From the tips of your toes to the top of your head *5*

3 The "rug" and you *7*

4 The ankle bone's connected to the shin bone *9*

5 The Greeks had a cure for it . . . *13*

6 Standing on your own two legs *15*

7 The Good Lord didn't intend it *that* way *19*

8 Four heads are better than one *25*

9 Hold that aching back *37*

10 It's what's up front that counts *45*

11 Take a deep breath *49*

12 The big reach *51*

13 On the cuff *59*

14 Proceed with caution *61*

15 Getting it together *65*

16 What it's all about *67*

17 Diet: The care and feeding of the engine *71*

18 The legs, your most important asset in sports *73*

19 The other fellow is even more tired *75*

20 Giving up today's pleasure for tomorrow's reward *77*

21 Ninety-pound weaklings are rarely all-Americans *79*

22 One after meals and one at bedtime *85*

23 Since they pay the bills . . . *91*

Index *97*

Introduction

Thirty thousand book titles a year is about average for publishing in the United States. And for every book there is probably a good—and different—reason for someone's having written it.

Our reason for writing *Conditioning for the High School Athlete* is to help young people toward healthier and more rewarding athletic careers. And for those who don't want to go as far as a "career," we hope it will help them achieve a healthier body and, as a result, a more optimistic outlook.

Conditioning for a young athlete requires just as much thought and application as though you were handling some professional superstar—a Reggie Jackson, a Tom Seaver, a Walt Payton, a Roger Staubach, a Julius Erving, a Rod Carew, a Jack Nicklaus, a Chrissy Evert, or any one of a half-dozen jockeys, who are among the highest paid athletes in sports.

The principles are the same, a regimen and sticking with it. And bringing the athlete to his maximum efficiency *before* any possible injury, so that the injury will be minimized in duration and effect.

The people who say nothing *really* changes, that it's just a new set of faces trying the old rules, really haven't kept up with the art of conditioning athletes. Things have changed in the business of bringing athletes to maximum efficiency and keeping them there. They've changed from fifty years ago and they've changed from five months ago. And they'll continue to change as dedicated persons strive to develop better ways of conditioning.

When Allan Webb was playing for the New York Football Giants and Dr. Allan Levy was becoming interested in the conditioning of high school athletes a couple of decades ago, the "duck walk" was standard practice. That's the "exercise" where you do a deep knee bend, keep it, and try to walk in that position—like a duck. And to make you really quack, how about a nice heavy weight balanced on your shoulders while en route?

You could try to think of a number of other ways to destroy a knee, but short of hitting it with a hammer, the duck walk is probably No. 1. What it does to the ligaments is something lamentable. Duck-walk a youth through high school and he becomes a prime prospect for knee trouble in college.

It used to be that "strengthening" the various parts of the body was rated more important than any other approach. Strengthen with weights, with isometric exercises, with isokinetic exercises. Yet within the past year irrefutable evidence has been developed that "strengthening" isn't nearly as important as "stretching" and "flexing." Today there are a number of teams in several pro sports who carry "flex" coaches. It's a job description that would have drawn a complete blank in sports in the late '60s.

The importance of a stretching and flexing program is matched only by the relative simplicity of its theory. It means that you're built up gradually to your maximum effort, and then returned to your normal condition equally as gradually. Example: In football, the quarterback begins by lobbing the ball at quarter-speed, then moves up to half-speed, then three-quarters speed, then full speed in time for either the practice session or the game. When the game or practice is over, he doesn't dash in to the shower but engages in a return to normal, throwing at three-quarters speed, then half, then a quarter.

It's the same with those who run. They build up from a jog to a sprint and come down the same way. This makes a great deal of sense: If you wind up a body, you have to wind it down. It's odd that it took about a hundred years of conditioning to figure this out.

All young boys try to do conditioning if they are athletic at all. They lift weights, they go out and run, they do exercises, they coax their families into buying those new fancy exercise machines. And they should be doing something if they are going to go into sports.

But the reason for our doing this book is to give them some kind of structured approach to what they should be doing. There are some things anxious young athletes do which are destructive; they might be better off sitting and reading a book.

This is not intended as an exercise book, but rather a book of approaches. There will be sections on prevention of injury, on mental attitudes, but we will always keep out front the idea that exercise is the basic need.

We'll be working with three types of exercises—isometric, isokinetic, and isotonic (weights). Allan Webb, responsible for the section of the book on weights, believes weights were what enabled him to pursue an athletic career, gaining him an athletic scholarship and giving him the physique to stand up under the stresses of a pro football career.

1
... and try not to get hurt

There is always the risk of injury in sports, particularly contact sports like football, hockey, wrestling, and basketball, although basketball's rule book indicates it is a noncontact sport. Doctors see a great many young persons of high school age with all kinds of injuries. A good portion of these trace to some basic weakness in a given area which, if corrected early, might have been prevented. Half of the injuries seen in this framework, if not preventable, could be minimized by proper conditioning.

If a boy plays on a regular team there is a time factor in connection with any injury he might come up with. In a nonathlete an injury that takes him out of 100 percent effectiveness for three weeks is annoying, but isn't disastrous. In a high school football player it's one-third of the season.

If a player is not only injured but out of condition, he may never realize his full potential. Thus, for our purposes there are two kinds of conditioning—one to enable an athlete to perform at his maximum, the other to keep him from being injured. And before going any further, it should be pointed out, keeping him from being injured is more important. *We are interested in building the body to its maximum to prevent injury.*

Earlier the three types of exercises were listed. *Isometric* means a maximum effort against an immovable object for a short time. A classic isometric example is standing in a doorway, hand flat against the side of the door frame, and bracing your back against the side. Nothing moves.

Isotonic means moving through a range of motion with effort. Isotonic exercises are basically those of lifting a weight through a range of motion for a particular muscle group.

Weight lifting and the Universal Gym so prevalent in the high schools are isotonic in type.

Isokinetics differ from isotonics in that the weight being moved through a range of motion varies in various positions. In isotonic exercise the weight load is always the same. However, as the muscle moves through a range of motion the mechanical advantage around the joint changes so that where the mechanical advantage is low the muscle is fully loaded but, as the advantage increases, the muscle is lifting progressively less than its limit.

In isokinetic exercise, due to the variable loading or eccentric cams in the weight-lifting machine, the weight varies through the range of motion so that the muscle is always completely loaded. It is felt generally that this is a better type of exercise but, since it requires expensive machinery, it is not always available. Machines of this type are the Nautilus equipment, the Orthotron, and now the Mini-Gym.

Sounds a little technical. Get down and do an old-fashioned pushup. Moving through a range of motion with effort. That's iso-TONIC. We know that the hardest part is getting the chest off the floor and that the pushup gets progressively easier as the arms straighten. If we could increase the body weight as we went up so it was equally hard all the way, it would be iso-KINETIC.

Iso-KINETICS and iso-TONICS are particularly good for lengthening muscles, for coordination, and for giving you a complete range of motion in the joints involved. Swimming and running are ideal isotonic exercises. Calisthenics provide isotonic activities but with limitations. Certain ones have been discarded. There are new machines available for working against stretching springs. On others you can set the resistance. There is none of this in isometrics. You can work one muscle group here against another set in the body, but no equipment is needed when you grab your own fingers and pull against them.

Flexing and stretching are a separate section and they do something no other exercise can—they prevent muscle pulls and tears. If you lengthen a muscle, it will perform better. Most warmup exercises in football and hockey are now stretching exercises. They've taken important things from ballet and modern dance and incorporated them into conditioning.

The most common injury—other than the bruise, which you can't do anything about—probably is the muscle pull. Simply stated, you get a muscle pull when a sudden severe force is applied to a muscle and it is stretched beyond its capacity to stretch. The fibers in the muscle actually tear.

The hamstring pull, which every athlete has heard about since the time he first put on a pair of pads or shoes, gets its name from the hamstring muscles in the thigh. The pull doesn't occur when you are pushing back on that hamstring muscle. It's when you throw your leg all the way forward, overextending it. Most pulls come from overextension in some way or other. If the minute fibers in the muscle tear, it's the so-called muscle *pull*. If the majority of the fibers tear, then you have the muscle *tear*. Obviously, a loose flat muscle isn't going to tear as quickly as a tight one. And, once you have a pulled muscle in your leg, there's no way you can run on it, no matter how much you want to.

Hockey players have strong ankles. We almost never see a hockey player with an ankle sprain because the act of skating itself strengthens the ankle. Exercise is very beneficial in treating an injury when it has occurred. The old theory was to stay off it. Now it's been found that "walking off" a sprain as soon as the pain allows, and exercising immediately thereafter, decreases the time needed for healing by 60 percent.

Serious injuries cut short careers, whether on the little league, high school, or college levels. Certain areas are particularly receptive to prevention of injuries with exercise. Almost all *minor* knee injuries can be prevented and at least half the major knee injuries made less serious.

The Good Lord didn't know about football when he designed the knee. It's fine for walking on it, running on it too, but it wasn't made to do the things that football and other sports demand of it. The knee wasn't made to withstand twisting motions with the knee bent. We've seen football players go out, plant their right foot, cut to the inside, go down in a heap, and never get up.

The knee isn't capable of making that twist when it's bent. It's not a socket but a shallow joint, like the shoulder, and not particularly well designed. We'll look into it in greater detail in subsequent chapters, but right now we must consider it to be the most important area in an athlete's body.

2
From the tips of your toes to the top of your head

Important as the knee is, it's not exactly at either end of the body. To keep some order in our thinking it's best that we start at one end and finish at the other; therefore, we'll treat each section of the athlete's and would-be athlete's physique from the feet up. The foot is the terminal part of the leg below the ankle joint on which the body stands and moves. It would be pretty difficult to go anywhere at a reasonable rate without a pair of them in reasonable working condition.

The foot's basic duty is to get you from one place to another, and to keep you from falling. It's the part of your body in contact with the ground. It is your propelling mechanism. Athletes are fond of describing them as your "wheels."

The foot is tremendously complex and takes a horrendous beating all your life. Just stop to think how many times your entire weight comes down on it in a given day. There are 1,800 foot strikes in each mile of jogging alone. It is a fantastic engineering structure with its bones, ligaments, arches, spring ligaments all put together so that some of us, gifted accordingly, can run a mile in under four minutes.

The foot is subject to many, many injuries, most of which we can't do anything to prevent with exercise. There are things like stress fractures, where one of the long bones simply cracks out of fatigue, just as a piece of metal will eventually give way to fatigue.

There are very few muscles of any particularly great strength in the foot. The important muscles there are those that move the toes and change the position of the foot.

There are two crippling foot injuries. The first is a sprain of the big toe, or "turf toe" as it is commonly known. This makes it impossi-

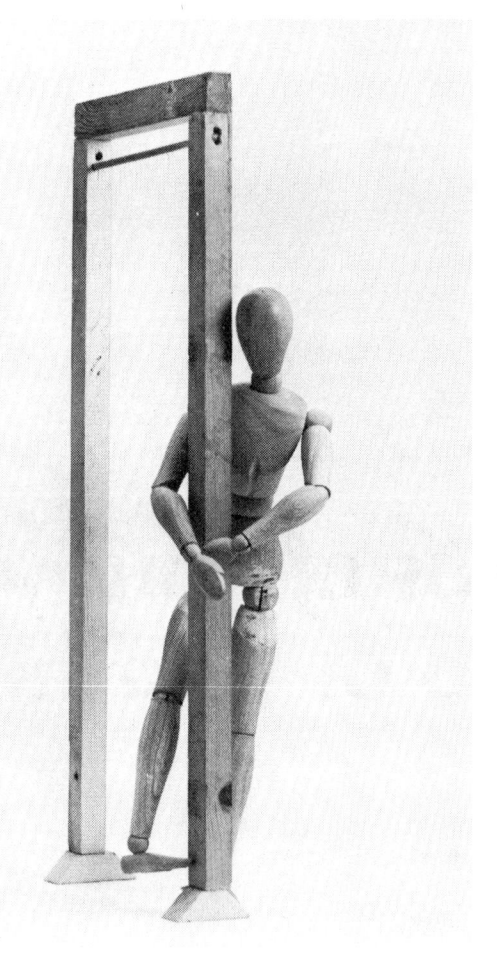

Figure 1. Place the foot against an immovable object such as a door frame or wall corner. Make maximum effort to turn the foot toward the inside against the wall. Hold for approximately five seconds.

Figure 2. Lateral isometric for foot and ankle. Procedure is the same as for the preceding exercise except the outside of the foot is placed against the wall and the pressure is directed outward.

ble to push off. The second is more serious, a tear of the arch of the foot, usually associated with an artificial surface. This is crippling for several months. As you go up the drive-train there are pulls and tears of all the structures. Incidentally, leg and back pain in older athletes is common for the whole season.

About the only foot injury that's preventable involves the arch. Of course, the way to beat it is to strengthen the arch, and one of the exercises used is toe-raising on a 2 x 4 piece of lumber. Place the lumber on its side on the ground. You put the ball of your foot on it, heel on the ground. Then you raise yourself on your toes. This exercise, like all others that will be listed in future chapters, calls for starting slowly and building up gradually.

If the 2 x 4's happen to be in short supply, the riser on the lip of a stair will do. Balance yourself on your toes off the edge of the stair and work from there. Make sure you pick the bottom stair so that if you have a mishap you don't have too far to fall.

This exercise can be used for the ankle and the Achilles tendon as well. It's one of the best methods of strengthening the arch and the foot. Another is picking up marbles with your toes. Running in sand, wet or dry, is still another. These are all forms of iso-KINETIC effort (moving through a range of motion, with effort, remember?).

3
The "rug" and you

No discussion of the foot is complete without a look into the merits of artificial surfaces, the most popular of which is Astroturf. It is a comparatively new development. It was unknown to the fathers of today's high school athletes. The all-weather playing surface has come to the fore in the last decade. Its popularity traces to the fact that you get pretty much the same conditions no matter what the weather. It is also a tremendous money-saver in the long run, a powerful factor whether you're talking about high school, college, or professional sports. If you can do away with three-quarters of your maintenance crew by the simple process of making a long-range investment—and artificial turf costs a lot of money—you tend that way, especially in an era when prices leap by healthy percentages from year to year.

We have seen a whole new batch of injuries in sports medicine directly relatable to artificial turf. And the finger is not being pointed at any particular brand. Research and study continue on the effects that playing on this type of surface might have on the various portions of an athlete's physique. It begins with the foot and extends clear up through the shoulders.

On any turf when you drive off you exert tremendous force against the ground. The entire energy in your body is concentrated into one relatively small area at a particular moment.

On regular turf, no matter how hard it happens to be from the sun or the cold, it'll give, even slightly. The cleats pack back into the turf. Some of your tremendous force is absorbed by this action, even if the "give" of the turf wouldn't be discernible to the naked eye.

In the union of the plastic or rubber sole of the shoe with artificial turf, there's simply *no give*. There can't be, because there's nothing to give. When you push off, the shock is immediately transmitted into your "drive-train" instead of some of it going backwards into the ground. The only situation remotely comparable is in basketball with rubber sneakers and wooden floor. But there isn't that tremendous drive off one foot in basketball, where quickness is more important than power.

It didn't take very long for a new type of athletic injury to develop once play began on artificial surfaces. They were largely injuries in the "drive-train" such as we had never seen.

The "drive-train," like in an automobile, is the body's power chain. It starts with the big toe, then proceeds through the arch of the foot, up the Achilles tendon and calf muscles, into the hamstrings and lower back. These are the structures that propel the athlete forward as he pushes off to run. All of these are subjected to pulls, tears, and other injuries on artificial turf.

Another big increase in artificial surface injuries has been in shoulder separations. We first thought it was the hardness of the turf, until we started to examine movies and discovered it wasn't that at all. It was due to the rubber pad under the artificial turf.

You came down hard on that shoulder and you bounced back up an inch or two. Then the second wave came along and drove you back down into it. That's where the injury came, on that second shot. On grass you're flat, no bounce, and you don't get that second blow.

A third and very real problem of artificial turf is the "burn," where the athlete leaves varying portions of his own outer covering on the artificial turf as a tribute to technical progress. This can largely be avoided if the players leave their sleeves long and try to keep their shirts inside their pants.

This is a problem in warm areas where short-sleeve shirts are of great value. Besides, some receivers simply can't catch a pass if they are wearing long sleeves. They need the "feel" of leather on their own skin, and they usually have to pay for this luxury. Sometimes the price of a pass catch comes very high.

If you're a ball carrier you can't help but get your hands torn up by the turf when you're tackled. The bent part of the wrist when you're holding the ball is particularly susceptible. Take a look at that area, plus the ball carrier's knuckles, during the season.

Surprisingly, there is also a high infection rate from these burns. We tend to think of a grass field as full of dirt, hence "dirty," but actually an artificial turf field is a lot more dangerous in this respect. It may look new and shiny but it is far from antiseptic. It can't be unless they scrub it with soap and water after every contest. Otherwise, it carries a high ratio of bacteria from the players themselves, as well as from other sources.

4
The ankle bone's connected to the shin bone

The regular dictionary description of the ankle will be sufficient for us. It is "the joint between the foot and the leg in which movement occurs in two planes." It is also, "the slender part of the leg above the foot."

The basic injury to the ankle is the sprain. Three fundamental types concern us—lateral, medial, and anterior. All three can be minimized because the ankle joint is held together by a number of fairly strong ligaments with muscles and tendons passing through the ankle to help support the ligamentous structures.

Lateral sprain: This occurs when the foot turns over to the outside. To set up the conditions, turn your foot so that the sole is pointing toward the other foot. Weight put upon it in this condition will tear the lateral ligaments. This is the commonest injury in basketball, and the commonest cause is when there is a pileup under the basket. Someone comes down on the side of someone else's foot and turns his ankle over to the side. It is the stepp*er* not the stepp*ee* who limps away from this one.

Medial sprain: This is much less common. It comes from rolling your foot to the inside. The reason it is less common is that the ligaments on the inside are stronger than those on the outside.

Anterior sprain: This happens when your toe gets caught and you go "over the top" of your own foot. A football player getting his toe cleats caught in the ground is a good example. It happens also in skiing. And baseball, where spikes are caught in a base. The anterior sprain is the most difficult of all three to heal.

The ligaments themselves can't be strengthened but the muscles around them can. A

10 Conditioning for the high school athlete

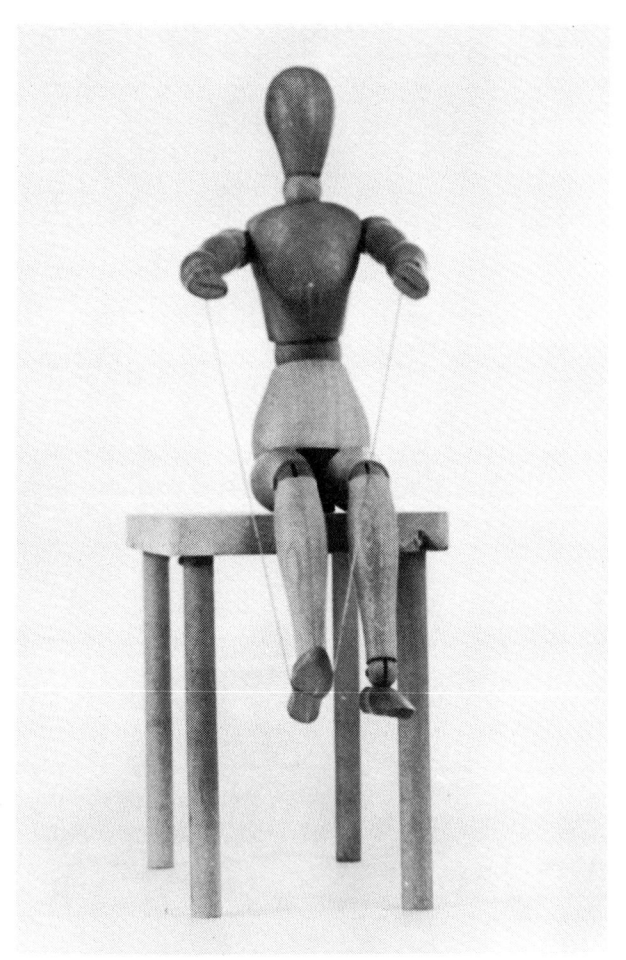

Figure 3. Wear rubber-soled shoes. Sit on a table: pass a piece of clothesline under the arch of the foot. Turn the ankle all the way to the inside and then apply pressure to the inside rope. A pull on the inside rope regulates the resistance against which the ankle is moved as it is turned all the way to the outside. When it reaches the full outside position, reverse the pressure and put it on the outside of the rope to force the ankle back to the inside. As strength in the ankle increases, the amounts of resistance on the rope can be increased.

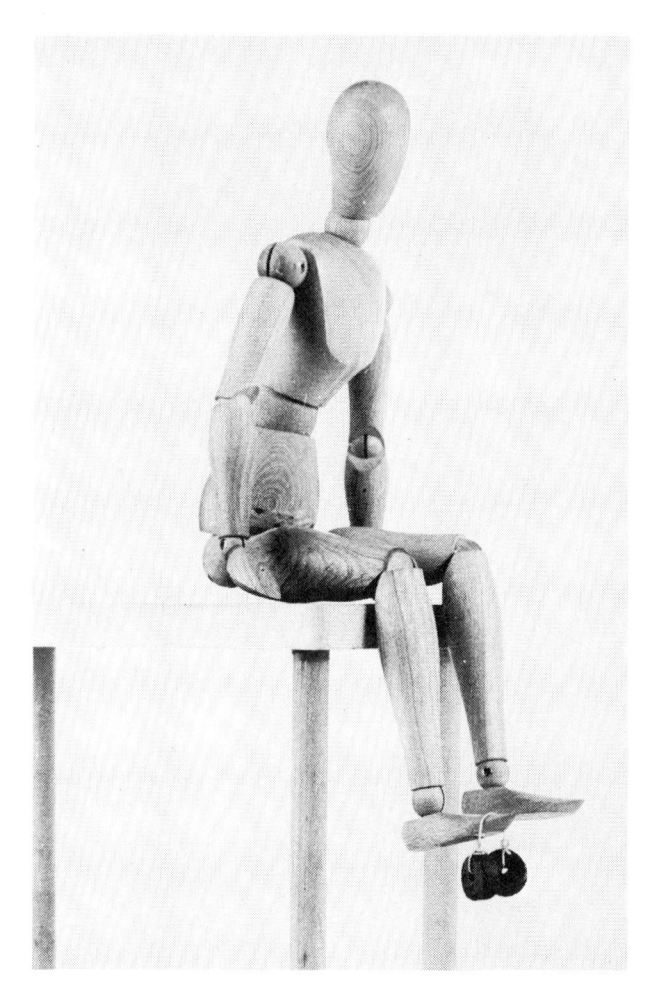

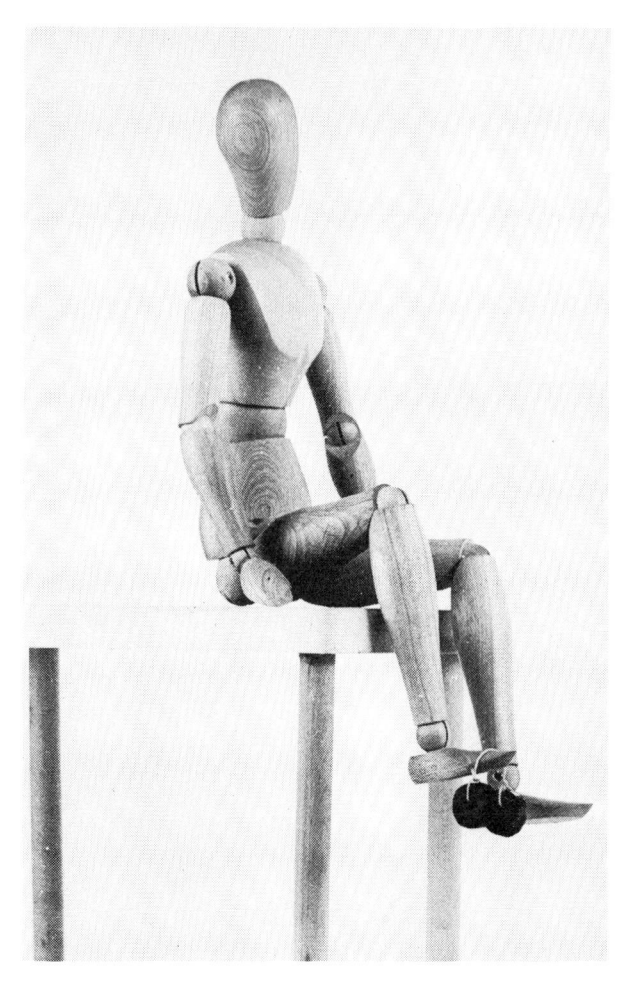

Figure 4. Anterior compartment toe weight. In this exercise, five-pound weights are attached to a short length of clothesline and hung over the break at the base of the toe. This can be done with the whole leg, as pictured, or just by flexing the ankle to raise the toes. It can be done to the point of fatigue.

good isometric exercise is to move the foot against an immovable object like a door jamb. To strengthen against an anterior sprain, catch your toe under an immovable object and attempt to lift. Toe weights of 2½ to 5 pounds can be used, tied together with a piece of clothesline over the base of the toes. This weight can be lifted for several minutes until fatigue is felt. In addition, working to the inside and outside of the ankle against the resistance of a piece of rope under the arch is of great benefit. (See figure 3.)

It's a good thought here to distinguish between ligament and tendon so that there's no confusion later. A ligament joins one bone to another. You've seen your father cutting through a ligament when he's separating a chicken leg away from the rest of the bird at the dining table.

A tendon joins a muscle to a bone. All muscles start and end at a bone. If you strengthen a muscle, you increase the tone of a tendon. The tendon *has* to get stronger if the muscle gets stronger because the muscle is pulling harder against the bone.

5
The Greeks had a cure for it...

Achilles tendon

The Achilles tendon, that very heavy tendon connecting the calf muscle to the back of your heel, a tendon that really *feels* like a tendon to the touch, is named after a legendary Greek hero who made quite a name for himself in the Trojan War. Early on, his mother, hearing a prophecy that he would eventually die in the fighting at Troy, attempted to make him invulnerable by bathing him in the River Styx.

Apparently only one immersion was permitted to a customer, so for the one quick plunge she held him by the heel. As a warrior he got Hector, who had killed his best friend, Patroclus, but was in turn nailed by Paris who got him with a poisoned arrow in his one vulnerable spot, his heel.

The vulnerability still exists for athletes but we can cut down on it considerably by conditioning.

The Achilles tendon exerts great force in running and lifting and it is responsible for the plantar flexion (sole) of the foot. Distance runners can strain their Achilles tendon. A tear in it is very serious and a tear all the way through, so that it is separated into two parts, is catastrophic.

An injury of this type will still permit you to walk on it because there are enough tendons involved, but you won't be able to run and you won't be able to raise yourself on your toes. Doctors, in seeing an Achilles tear, have come to expect to hear, "I was running and someone kicked me in the back of the heel and knocked me down." That is precisely what it feels like and it's a good description, except that the injured athlete frequently will have been all by himself when it happened.

An Achilles tendon tear is a difficult one to fix. Surgery is involved and the foot must be in a cast during the recuperative period. The best thing is to try to strengthen the area as much as possible to prevent trouble.

The basic Achilles exercise is the toe raise and heel drop from the stairs. The 2 x 4 that you used earlier for the ankles comes in handy here. Turn it the other way so that you're working on the four inches of height. You want to get as far back down with your heel as you can. And remember, use that bottom step as you did in the earlier exercise. When doing the toe raise previously described, allow your weight to take your heels as far down as they can stretch and hold.

You also can walk around on your heel with your toe in the air. The important thing is stretching, because a short tendon always has a greater tendency toward injury than a long one. You're stretching the muscle around it to take the pressure off the tendon and permitting it to relax. Walking around barefooted will help because your foot wasn't designed to wear shoes, but there's a danger here of puncture and lacerations. Walking barefooted you tend to grip more with your toes and that's a good thing.

A word here about the current fad of high heels in men's shoes. Like high heels in women's shoes, this fashion has nothing to recommend it from the health standpoint. Women who have worn high heels over a period of years find they are unable to walk in flat shoes without pain. That's because the Achilles tendon has become shortened.

There's no difference between men's and women's feet as far as the Achilles tendon is concerned and it's strongly recommended that athletes, and everyone else, stay away from high heels. If some athletes find them irresistible, they should be sure to counterbalance this with plenty of Achilles tendon stretching. It seems too big a price to pay—a serious leg problem in the future—for a little fancy dressing today.

6
Standing on your own two legs

For purposes of conditioning, the leg is divided into two compartments, the front (anterior) and back (posterior). Both are extremely important to the athlete.

The muscles in the front part of the leg have as a function the raising of the front of the foot, This is the motion that occurs in walking and running as you bring the foot forward to bring it down.

The most common injury here, and one of the most difficult to treat, is the "shin splints." It cuts down the athlete's effectiveness drastically, and it has a tendency to linger.

What causes shin splints is open to controversy. Probably it is a pulling away of the capsule around the bone, caused by jarring. Little hemorrhages occur under it. The pain is along the big bone of the lower leg.

The injury undoubtedly has something to do with continual pounding on a hard surface. It is seen more in basketball (hardwood floor) than in football (dirt field). A universally recommended preventative treatment is the Achilles tendon stretching described earlier. This exercise contracts the muscles in front of the leg for stability. If shin-splints become a persistent problem, in spite of Achilles tendon stretching, they are usually due to improper foot balance and improper foot strikes. These are correctable by orthopedic devices worn in the running shoe which have to be handmade to the individual's foot.

The posterior compartment, or back of the leg, has two very heavy muscles needed for pushing off on your foot. As you run forward, you come up on your toes and push off from the foot. This is accomplished by the big bunchy muscle in the back of the calf, the

16 Conditioning for the high school athlete

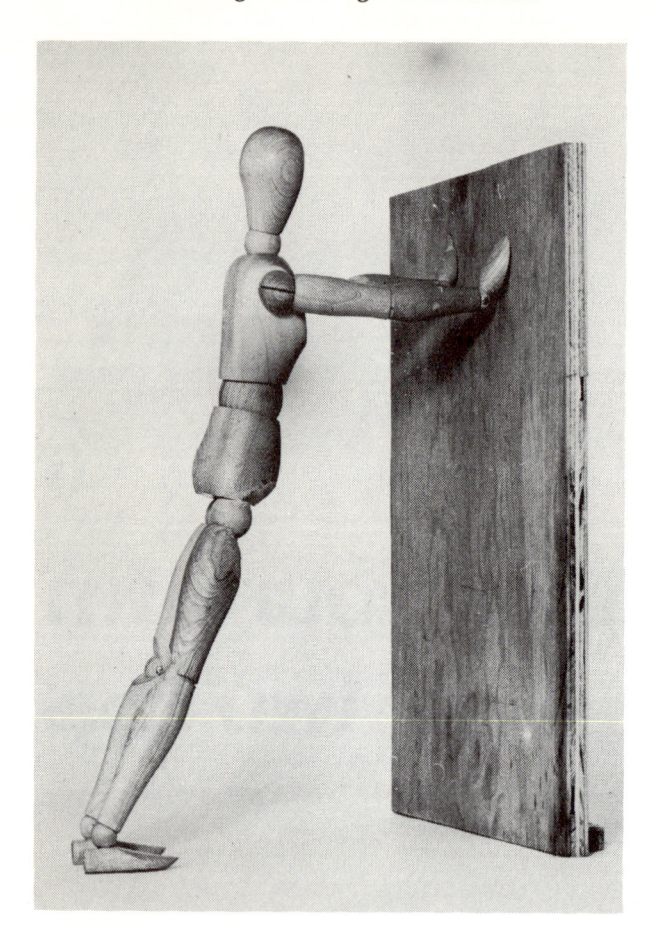

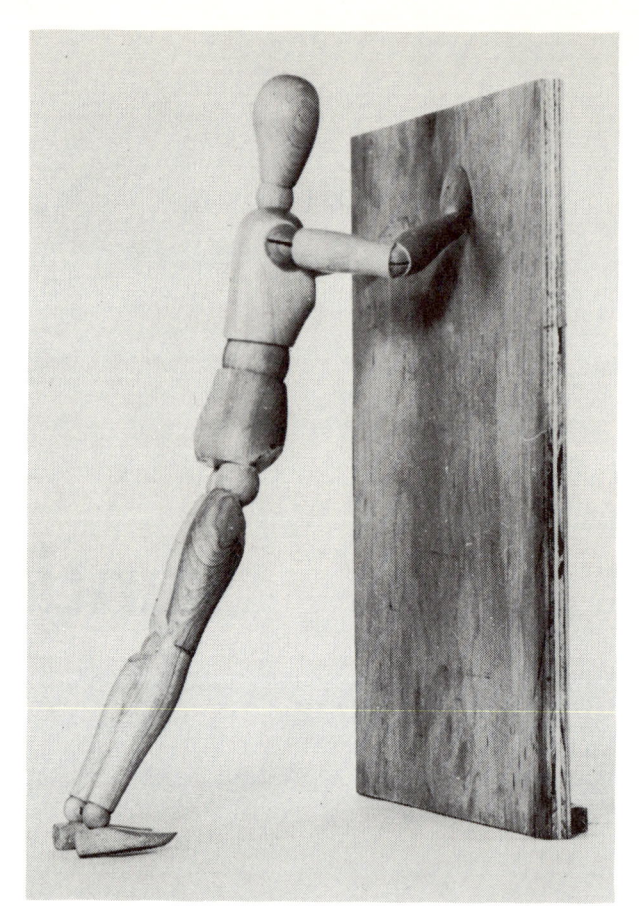

Figure 5. Gastroc and Achilles stretch. The gastrocnemius is the cell muscle that attaches to the Achilles. This exercise is done leaning against a wall as pictured. With the heels flat on the floor the body is let down as in a push-up until strain is felt in the back of the legs. This is maintained from eight to ten seconds. The basic exercise is done with toes pointing straight ahead.

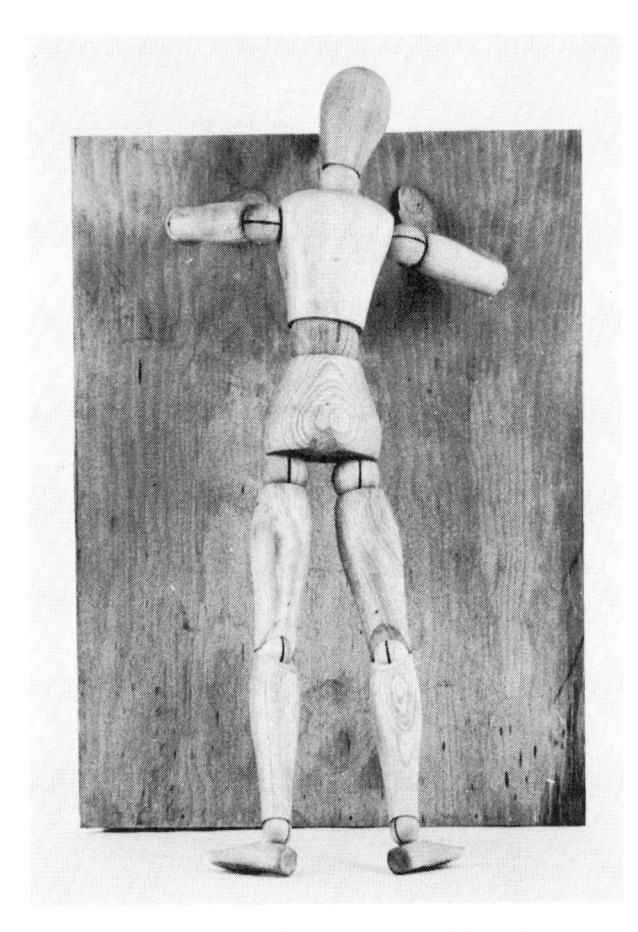

Figure 6. Gastroc stretch in eversion. This is the same exercise with the toes pointed out, away from each other. This stretches the inside of the calf muscle.

Figure 7. Gastroc stretch in inversion. This is the same exercise with the toes pointed toward each other in a pigeon-toed fashion. This puts the stretch on the outside of the calf muscle.

gastrocnemius. If you do any running, you really don't have to worry about strengthening these muscles. They're going to be strong.

The problem exists, though, in preventing tears and pulls. Most of the power muscles in the leg have to be lengthened, rather than stretched.

Stretches are done with the foot flat on the floor. The athlete leans forward, bracing himself against the wall, letting himself slide forward to the wall. At arms length, this is like a pushup if you were flat.

You also stretch in inversion. This means the toe is pointed in and the foot is rolled around on the outside. *Eversion* is with the toes pointed *out* duck-fashion, with the rolling done on the *inside* of the foot.

This exercise will also stretch the Achilles tendon. All the stretches should be done slowly—without any jerking, without any forcing—and must be maintained for a period of about 20 seconds. The only way you're going to lengthen a muscle fiber is by putting a gradual stretch on it for a prolonged period of time.

7
The Good Lord didn't intend it *that* way

The knee is the joint that allows for movement between the femur and tibia and is protected by the patella.

Among sports people, trainers, coaches, and the medical personnel assigned to take care of the players, it's generally agreed that the knee is the most important, and most vulnerable, portion of the body. It is also generally agreed that sports call for the knee to do things for which it never was intended. So we are in an area of continual compromise and the best we can hope to do is to strengthen the knee so that minor injuries will be avoided and major ones minimized.

The knee was made to bend only one way. Just bend your knee while you're sitting and reading this. That's the one way! Any other way, if enough pressure is applied, will damage the knee. Damage it enough and the sports career is over.

The knee is controlled by two sets of muscles, front and back. The major set is in front and is called the quadriceps femoris. It consists of four muscles with one common muscle mass known as quadriceps. This muscle comes down and inserts on the inside and outside of the knee. In addition to that, a large part of the muscle becomes the quadriceps and patellar tendon which encompasses the knee cap and is the only muscle responsible for straightening the leg from the bent position.

Loss of function in the quadriceps will result in all kinds of pains, aches, and actual rocking of the knee. Strengthening it will result in a strong, durable knee where minimal problems will develop. It is the key to the healing of a damaged knee. It takes over the holding of the knee together and allows the ligament which may have been bumped or damaged to rest.

The hamstrings do the same thing in the back of the knee. They must be strengthened to hold the knee together from the posterior aspect. They come down and divide on either side of the knee in the back. The quadriceps will lose girth within three days of a knee injury, hence the importance of over-developing this area.

How do we do this? A number of ways are open, but one that *must be avoided* is deep-knee bends. The reason is simple. They tear down the knee rather than build it up, which will come as quite a shock to generations of trainers who leaned heavily on this nonsense. It's nonsense because we know now that a deep-knee bend causes tremendous strain on the ligamentous structure. Use of weights while doing so compounds the damage. The "duck waddle," used as a kind of punishment for athletes who loafed, etc., was one of the greatest culprits in this connection.

Any exercise to the knee should *never* go below a half-bend, especially the weight programs. It's hard to get old-timers to break their habits, but there is no place for the deep-knee bend anywhere in a training regimen.

What are these ligaments that the deep-knee bend is bound to damage as certainly as being hit from the outside with the leg set and planted on the ground? The knee is held together by five major structures. The medial ligament goes down the inside of the knee connecting the two bones. The lateral ligament does the same thing on the outside of the knee. Two crossed ligaments, called the cruciates, act the same way as crossed supporting planks that hold up a wall. They are deep inside the knee under the patella.

One runs from the front part of the lower bone to the back part of the upper bone. The other runs from the back part of the lower bone to the frontal part of the upper bone. They keep the knee from sliding forward and backward.

The lateral and medial ligaments prevent the knee from breaking to the side or the middle. And, finally, there is the posterior capsule, the lining around the back of the knee, which is also a very strong structure.

The most common injury to the knee in sports comes when it is subjected to a blow on the outside while the heel is fixed to the playing surface. Something has to give, as the old song said, and it's this irrevocable law of physics that keeps orthopedic surgeons busy Monday mornings during the football season. This injury is most common in football because that sport uses the deepest spikes.

If the heel is free and can rotate to the inside when the knee is hit from the outside, it will disseminate the force and the knee will simply rotate away from the impact. If the foot is fixed, the knee has no place to go except to break open on the inside, which sprains or tears the medial ligament. In addition, the medial ligament is attached to the medial cartilage and, if the medial ligament goes, the medial cartilage usually goes, too. Even if the medial ligament stretches without actually tearing, it can tear the medial cartilage loose.

We see this same condition in rare cases on the outside when someone's head makes contact with the inside of the knee. The lateral ligaments on the outside, however, are not attached to the lateral cartilage so lateral cartilage tears are less common. As the force increases to the knee, depending on how wide apart you force the inside of the knee, first the medial ligament gives way; secondly, the medial cartilage tears; then the anterior cruciate ligament goes.

We now have a knee that's unstable, backward and forward, in and out. This is the "Terrible Triad of O'Donohoe," named after an outstanding orthopedic surgeon. It's the knee which, when it is laid open for surgery, looks as though an explosion had taken place inside.

Now to the optimistic side, and everything has an optimistic side. By exercise and strengthening the surrounding structures of the knee, we can cut out completely or minimize 70 percent of the knee injuries that ordinarily hold someone out for three or four days. And with proper shoes and playing surfaces we can minimize a certain percentage of the major knee injuries.

There are, of course, the nonpreventable injuries in the knee department, just as in others. No matter what you do, there's going

The Good Lord didn't intend it that way 21

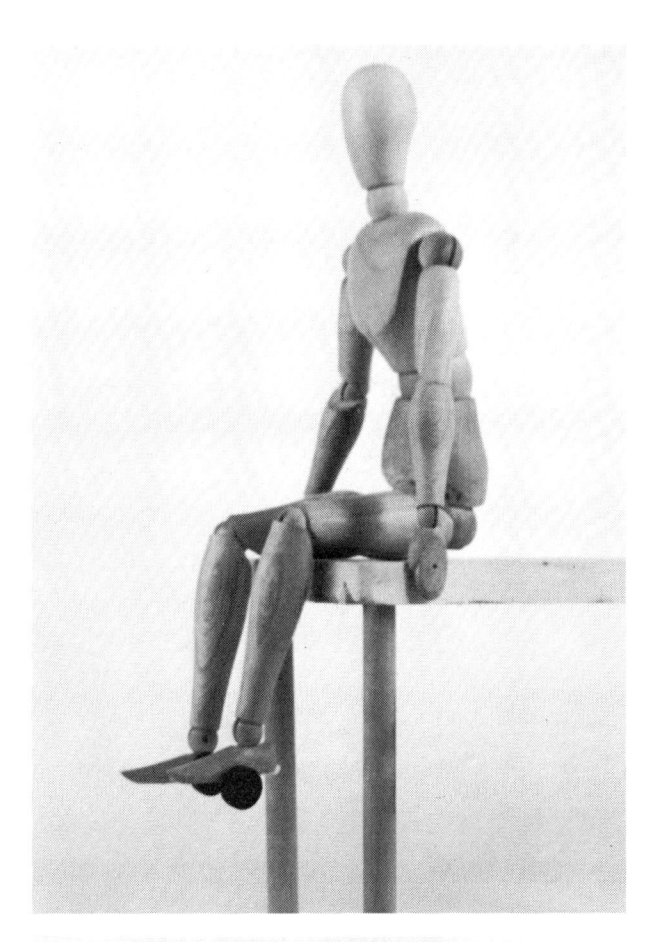

Figure 8. Quadriceps strengthening with weights. Sit on the edge of a firm table with a weight boot or sand in a canvas tote bag attached to the foot. Straighten knee to full extension, hold for three seconds, then drop. Five sets of ten lifts can be done until extreme fatigue occurs.

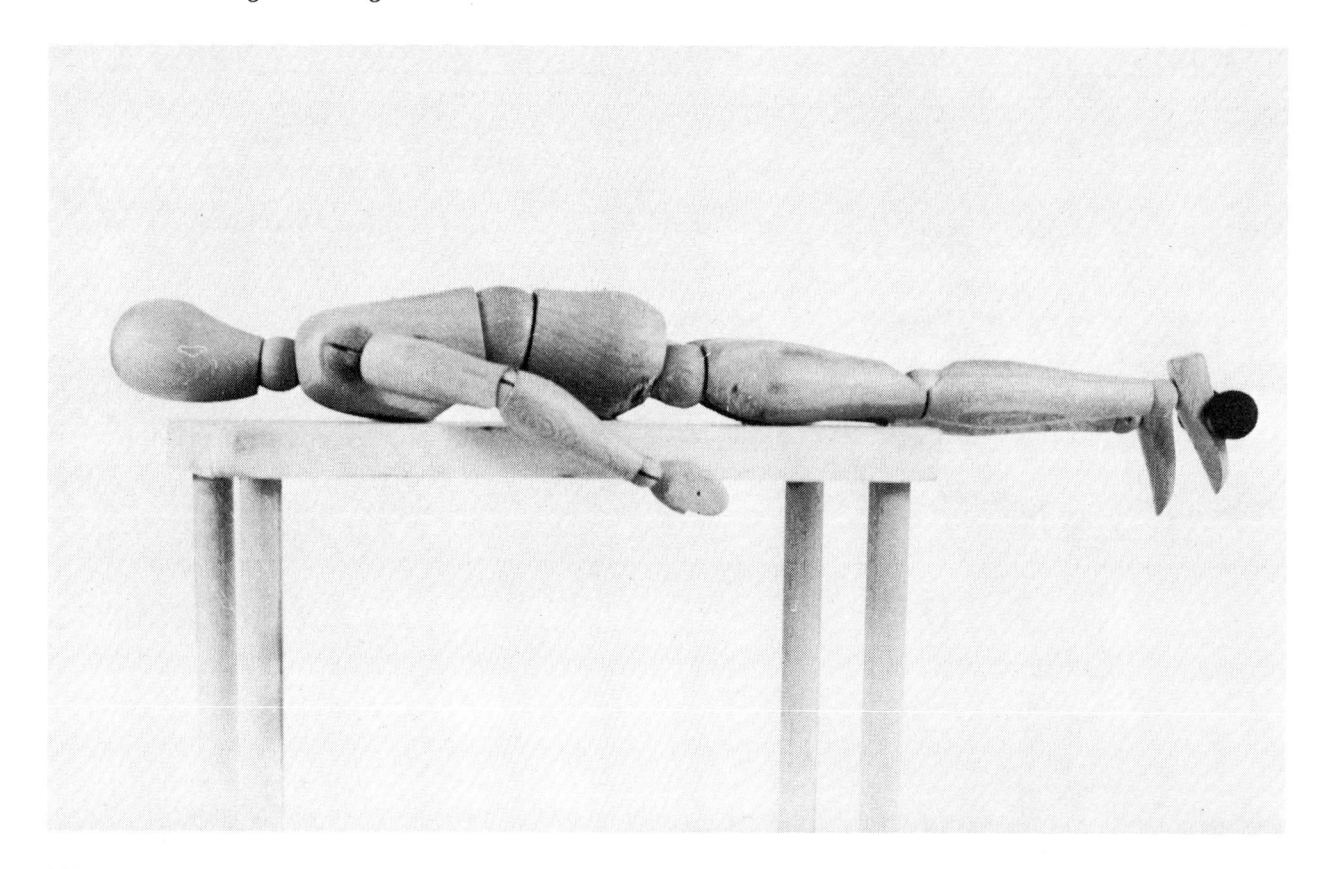

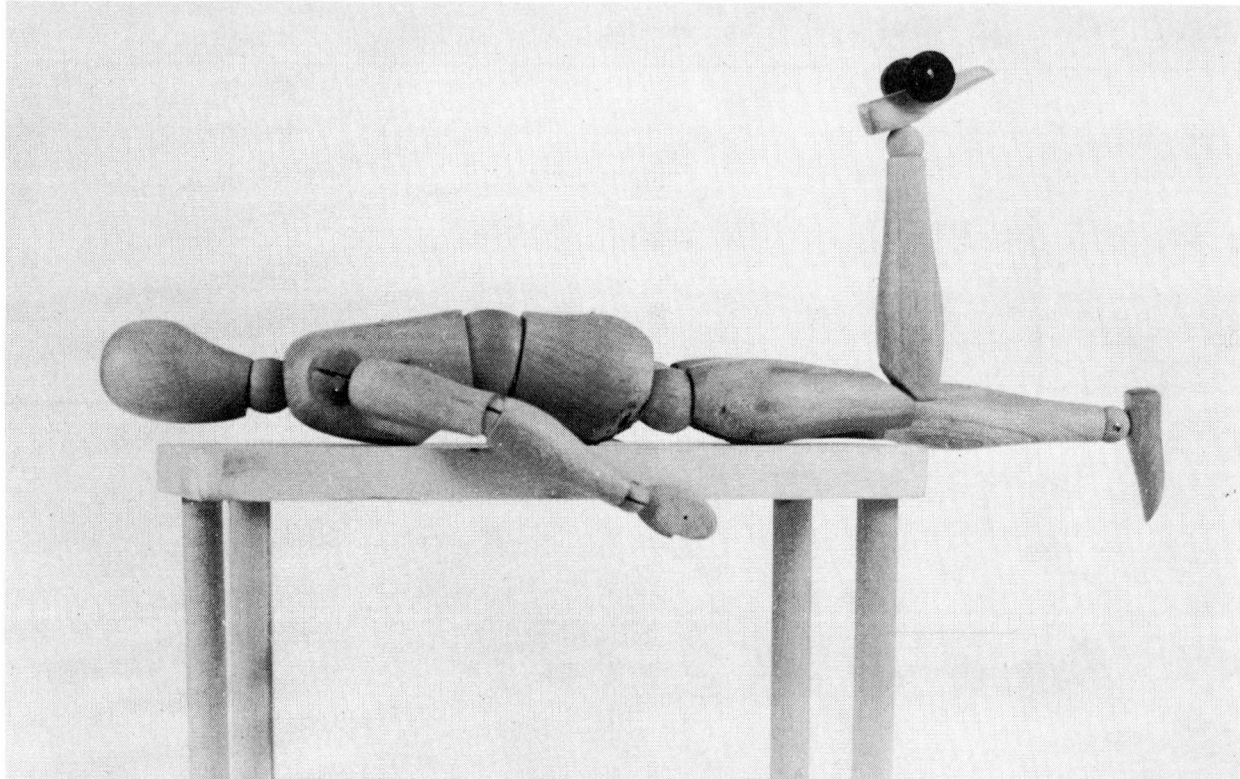

Figure 9. Hamstring lift. This exercise is done lying on the table with the weight boot or weight and lifting at the knee to 90 degrees. Again, five sets of ten should be done.

to be the dry-twig injury, where a player goes down in a pile-up, his knee is suspended across two others players and someone falls on top. It's like taking a dry twig and laying it across two stones and stamping on it with your foot. It's simply going to break. Nothing you can do will prevent it.

Beginning our program of strengthening the knee, we approach the isometric quadriceps first. This calls for a maximum contraction of the quadriceps muscle. With the leg fully extended you make an effort to pull the knee cap up toward the hip. It doesn't have to be held long.

It should be done and held for one or two seconds. Relax and repeat, and do it in runs of 50. You can stand and do it once you get control. It shouldn't take more than a minute and a half to do 50.

There is also the graduated weight program which is done with either the universal gym or a weighted boot. The athlete sits on the end of the table, extends his leg fully and locks the knee. It is in the last 15 degrees of elevation that you're assisting the quadriceps. The leg is held in full extension for three seconds. You determine the maximum amount of weight you can lift when you're fresh.

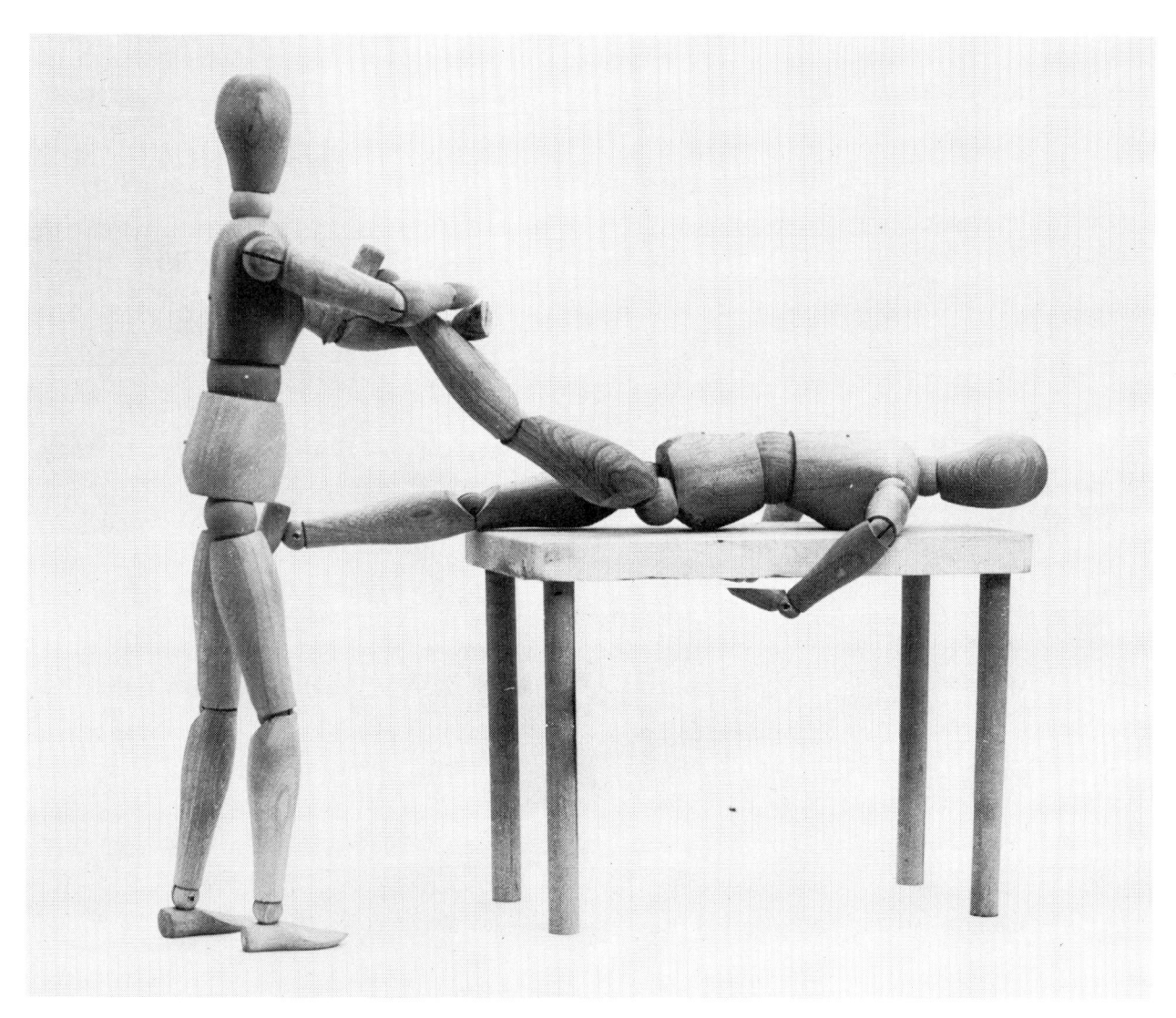

Figure 10. Hamstring lift with partner. Lie on the stomach on a table. Lift the leg against the resistance of a partner. Maximum effort should be held for eight to ten seconds.

Suppose you learn that your maximum lift is 60 pounds. Therefore, start with 25 percent of that (15 pounds) ten times. Go to 50 percent, and repeat the same thing immediately. Then to 45 pounds. At this weight you probably won't be able to do ten lifts because the leg has to be getting tired by now.

Then go to 100 percent. You probably won't be able to do any at all at this weight because the leg is now fatigued, but don't be disheartened. By repeating the program every day, in a week or ten days you'll be doing all ten lifts. On the next day after you've done this maximum weight ten times, boost the maximum weight by ten pounds and repeat the entire program, boosting each stage by the same percentages.

If you work on a machine rather than with a weighted boot, do each leg independently rather than together, because if there's any weakness in either leg, the good leg will be doing all the work.

Then it comes time to turn onto your stomach and do the same exercises using the hamstring muscles. You assume a fully extended position either on the table or floor and work toward a 90-degree rise at the knee. In other words, the foot will be directly up in the air. It isn't necessary to hold this, because at this point no weight will be supported by the hamstring muscles. So, this exercise can be done with no "hold" at the top, just up and down. The same percentages program—25, 50, 75, and full—is used.

In the absence of weights, both the quadriceps and the hamstrings can be exercised with a partner. You work against the resistance supplied by the partner. No percentage program is possible here.

On the weight machine, the leg press is used. The legs are pulled up to the body, then fully extended, working against the weights.

8
Four heads are better than one

The thigh

Injuries to the thigh are sustained either in the front or back. The basic injury in front is to the quadriceps muscle. This is the large four-headed muscle that controls the knee. Such an injury is a "charley horse," a hemorrhage due to a tear or trauma. The quadriceps is one of the two or three muscles in the body that have the peculiar property of forming calcium. When this happens it is very disabling. The calcium will probably dissolve in a period of a year, but surgical removal is sometimes necessary. Therefore, it is important to protect the quadriceps.

An excellent exercise here is the "crane." You stand on one leg, the other leg straight out behind you. Grab your ankle with your hand and slowly pull up to stretch the front of your leg. You'll know you're doing it properly if you feel the pull. Strengthening exercises are covered in the section on the knee, Chapter 8.

The back of the thigh is subject to hamstring pulls and tears. This is where the drive in running comes from. There are a half-dozen methods for stretching this area. Again, strength exercises are covered in Chapter 8 under the knee. Stretching is of utmost importance, because the hamstrings pull easily.

The toe grab is best. Bending your knee to get down in a crouch, grab your toes so that your fingers are under your foot all the way to the knuckle. Slowly straighten your knee until you begin to feel that pull. Do this 20 seconds at a time.

The next exercise is the forward bend on a chair. You put your leg straight out on a chair, then bend forward trying to touch your knee or ankle.

Figure 11. Crane stretch. Grasp the leg at the ankle and bring up and back so that there is maximum stretch on the upper thigh and hip. Maintain for ten seconds.

Figure 12. Forward bend on chair. Place the ankle on the back of a chair or table. Make an effort to bring the head down to meet the leg.

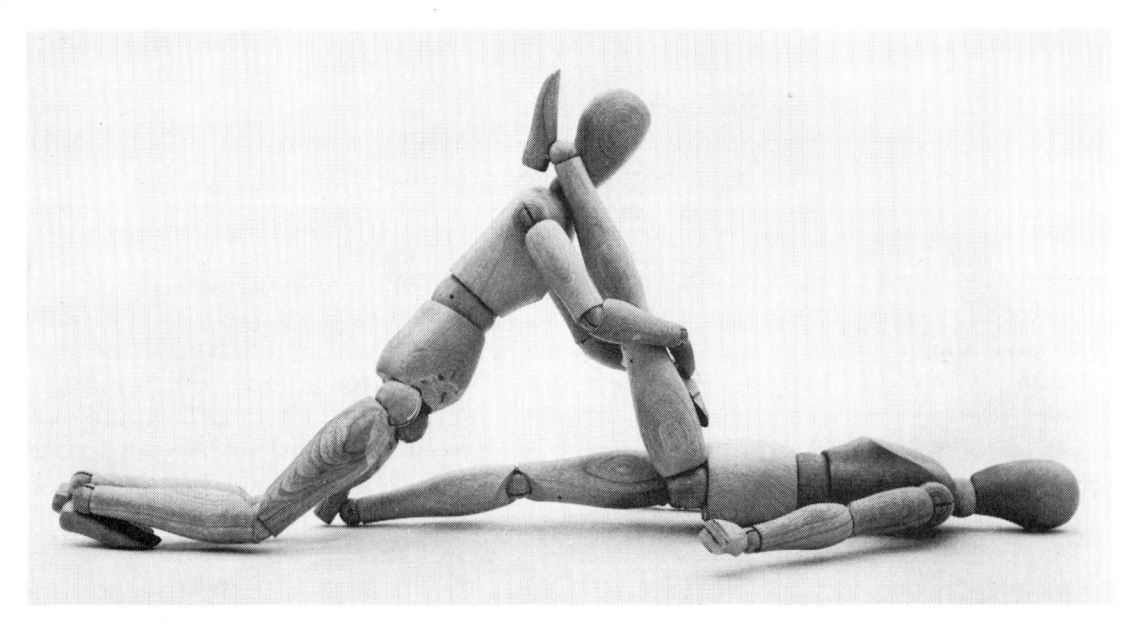

Figure 13. Hamstring stretch with partner. On the ground or low table, place the foot over the partner's shoulder. The partner keeps the knee straight and the hip is flexed to point of maximum stretch of the hamstrings.

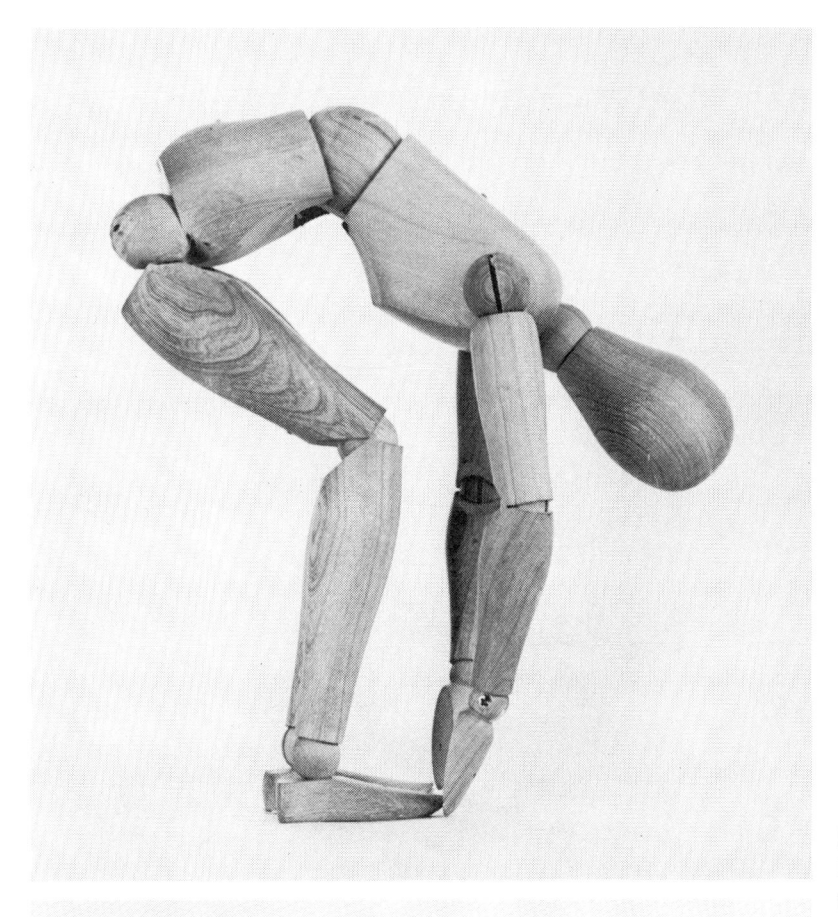

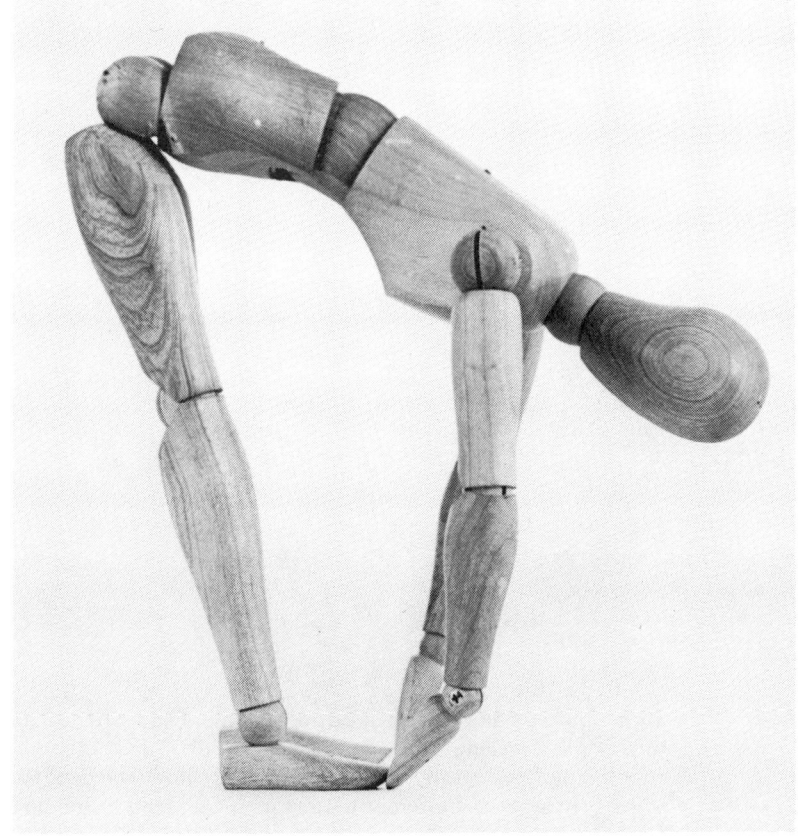

Figure 14. The grab stretch. Bend the knees. Place hands all the way to the palm under the soles of the feet. Then gradually straighten knees until there is a marked pull in the hamstring area.

28 Conditioning for the high school athlete

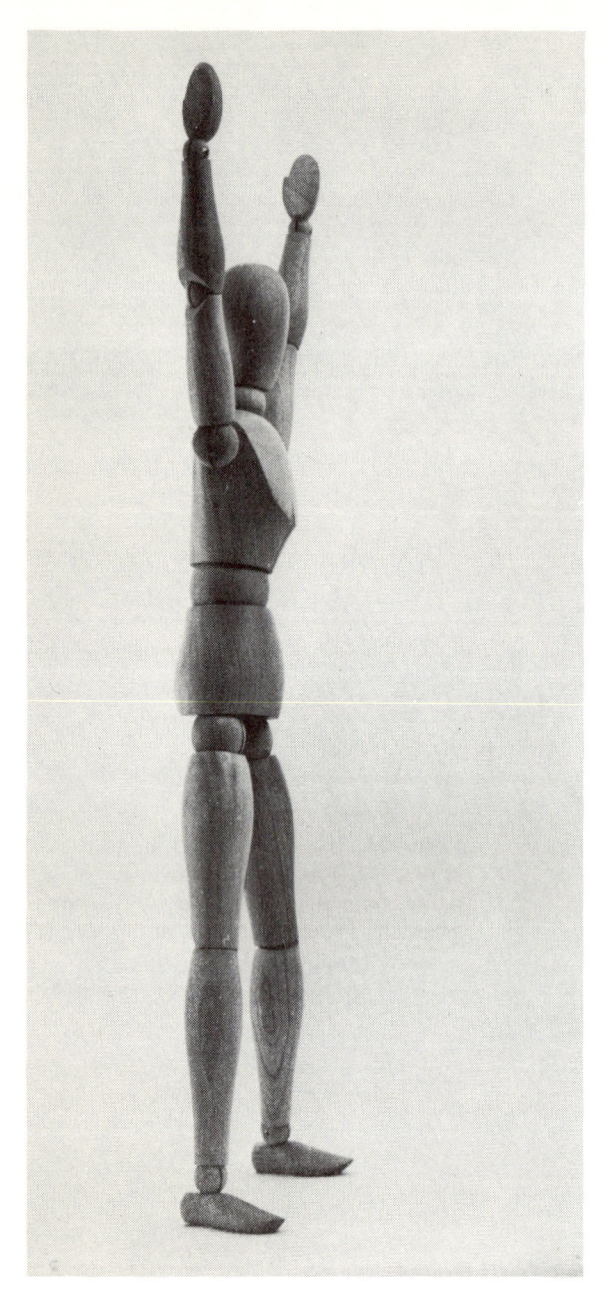

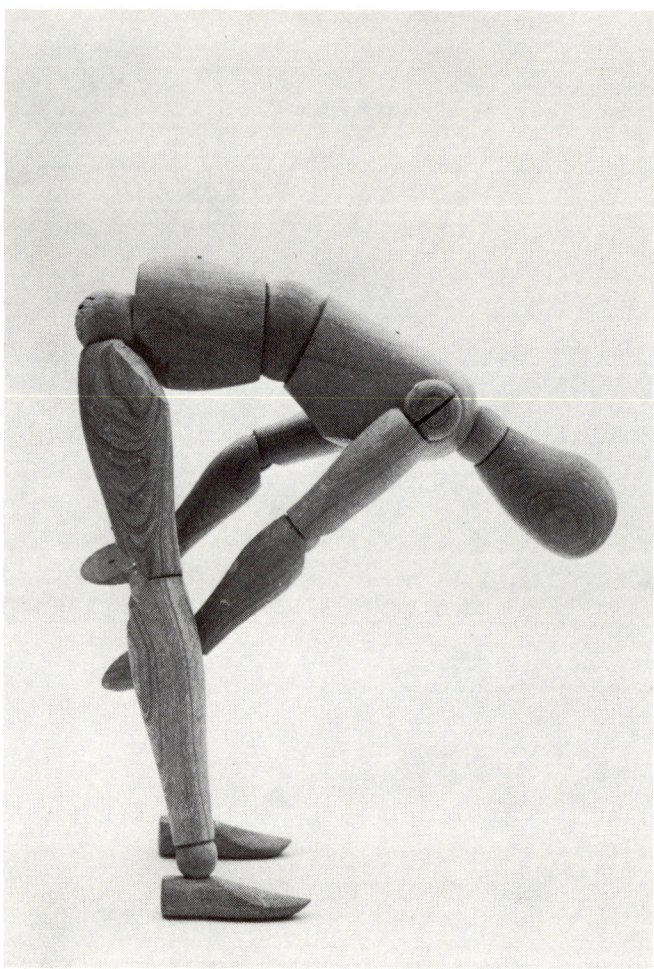

Figure 15. Start with hands above the head and back arched, full extension. Bend rapidly. The exercise ends with the head and hands bending all the way through the open legs to the back.

Figure 16. Hurdler's stretch, opposite page. Place one leg forward and one leg trailing in the hurdler's position. The exercise begins by rocking back on the back leg and stretching. The second part is a full forward bend attempting to touch the head to the ankle in a stretch.

Four heads are better than one 29

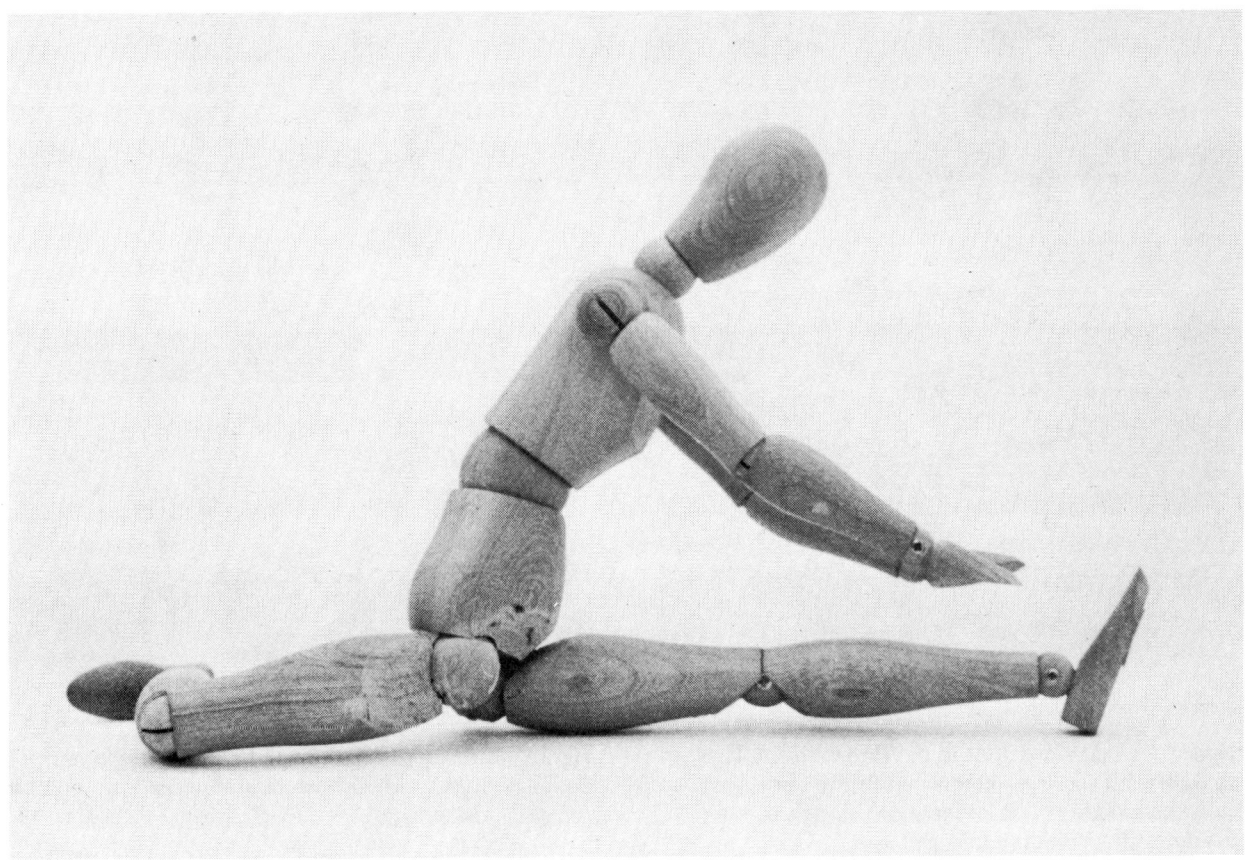

Another exercise is to do the work with a partner. Lie on your back on the ground. Raise your leg, placing your heel on your partner's shoulder. He is facing you. He locks his hands on your knee, then moves his shoulder forward. This is just fine, provided you have a partner who stops when you start experiencing severe pain and doesn't keep going, trying to tear your hamstring in half.

Figure 17. Place one foot to the side with the leg straight with the foot maintained in the same spot, shift the weight to the other leg to stretch out the inside of the straight leg.

He has to feel the resistance and know when to stop.

The woodchopper exercise with a posterior reach is also effective. With your legs spread apart you raise your hands over your head and come straight down between your legs as though you were trying to chop something with an ax. Follow through as far as you can.

The crossed-toe is the same exercise, except it is done with your feet crossed.

The last is the famous hurdler's stretch. It is important here that there is no jerking. Many athletes have short hamstrings and will expe-

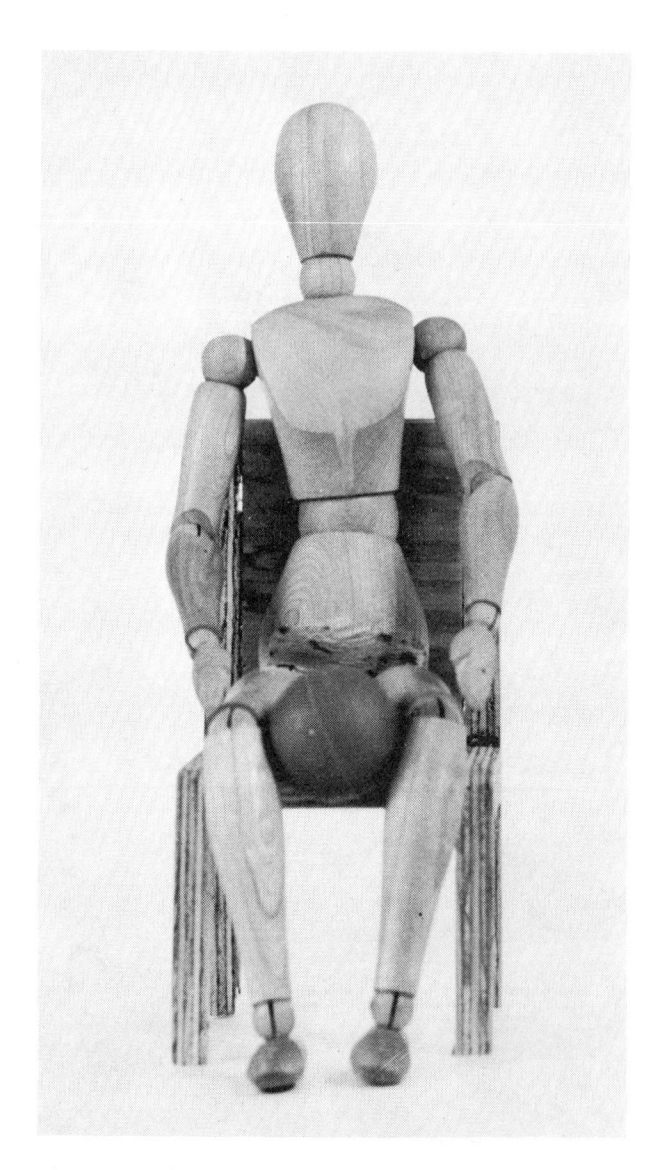

Figure 18. Place the basketball between the knees. Squeeze firmly and with maximum effort from eight to ten seconds.

Four heads are better than one   31

Figure 19. Supine leg windmill. Lie on your back. Start with the legs together and raised to 90 degrees, then open to the outside and bring them back together again.

32 Conditioning for the high school athlete

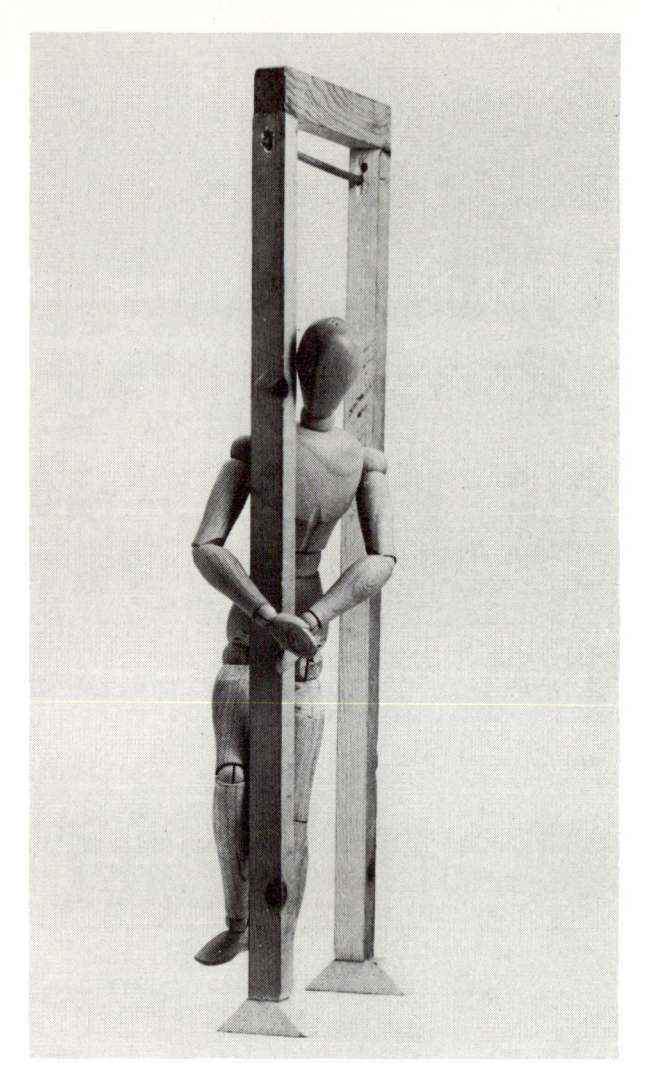

Figure 20. Medial isometric for groin. Place the inside of the knee against the door jam. Exerting maximum effort, bring the knee to the inside.

Figure 21. Sit in the yoga lotus position, with the hands or the elbows placed on the insides of the knees and the knees spread toward the floor.

rience continuous trouble such as back problems unless something is done to lengthen them. The hamstrings are attached to the pelvis and, if they aren't lengthened, they tend to roll your pelvis forward and this unnatural position tends to set up backaches.

The groin

The groin is that area where your leg joins your body. An injury here probably means you can't run, and there is really nothing you can do except wait for it to get better. We see it in all sports, but it is particularly common in hockey where the skate slips suddenly to one side on the ice. The area can be strengthened isometrically and isokinetically. In isometric work the leg is placed against the door jamb or wall. The leg is bent, the knee is pushed against the door jamb and is brought in. Another exercise is to place a basketball between the legs and squeeze. Lots of young hockey players in Canada have basketballs and use them solely for this purpose.

In the isotonic department you do the windmill on your back. With your legs up, wave them back and forth.

The groin can be strengthened by stretch-

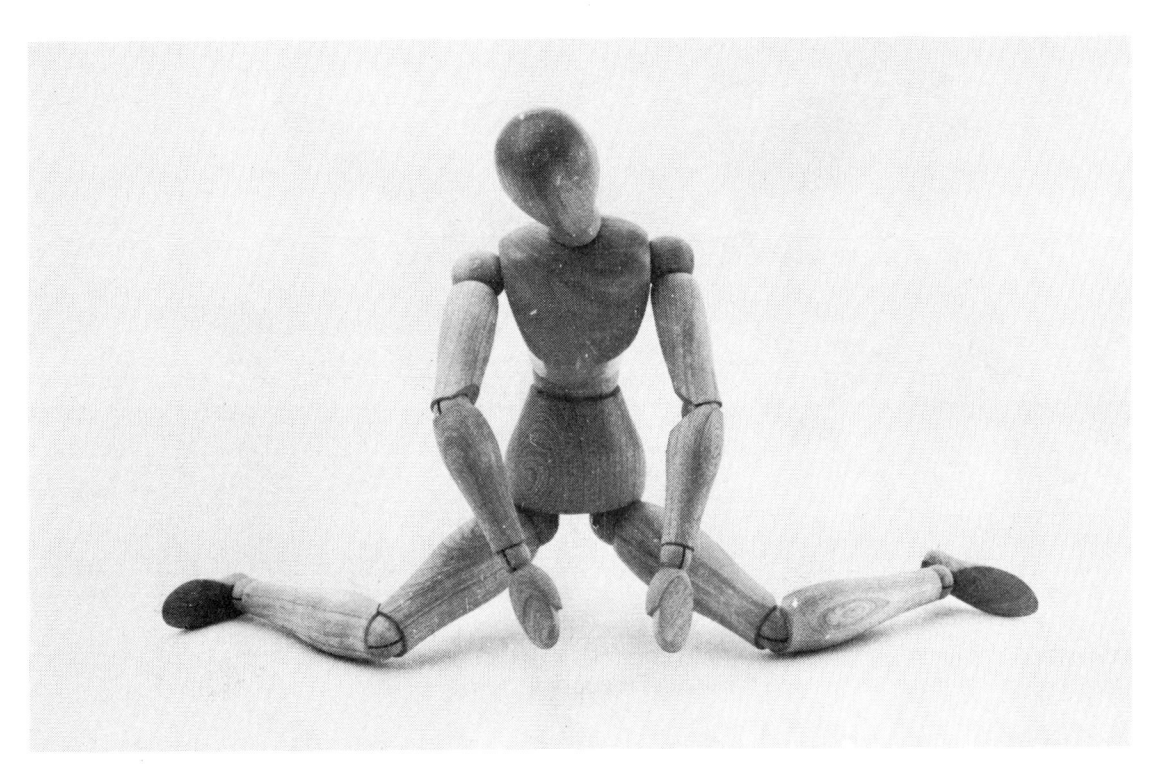

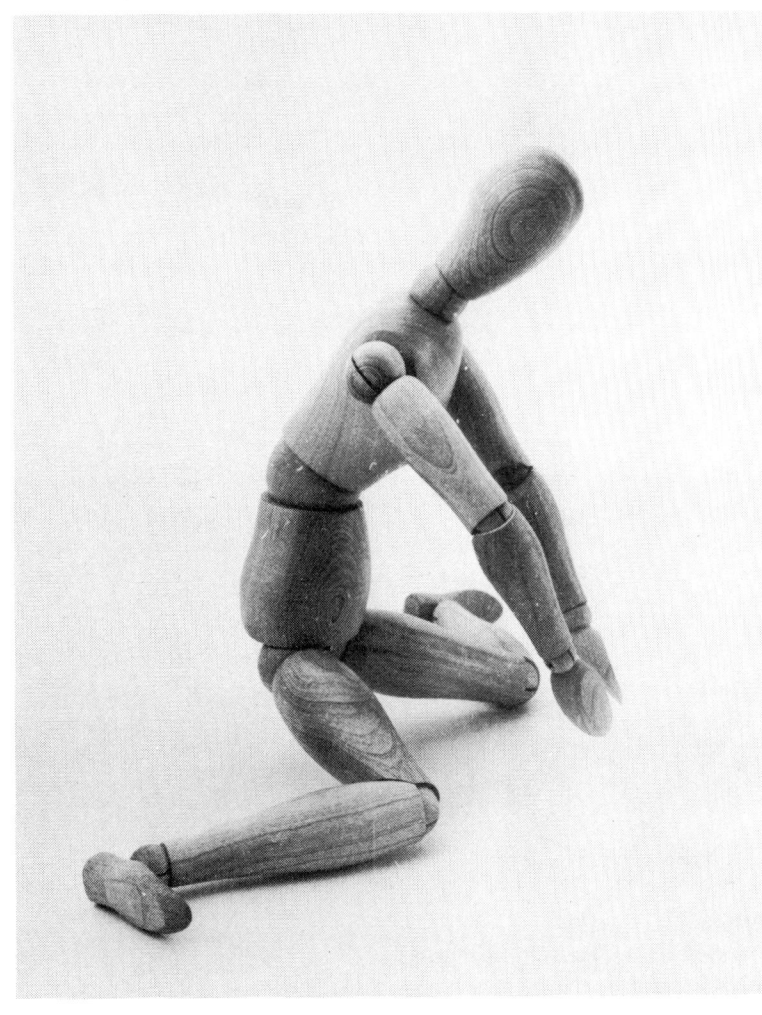

Figure 22. With the feet directly out to sides and the knees spread, stretch the groin by rocking forward.

34 Conditioning for the high school athlete

Figure 23. Assume the position of the runner's start by rocking forward. Stretching can be applied to the trailing leg in the area of the groin.

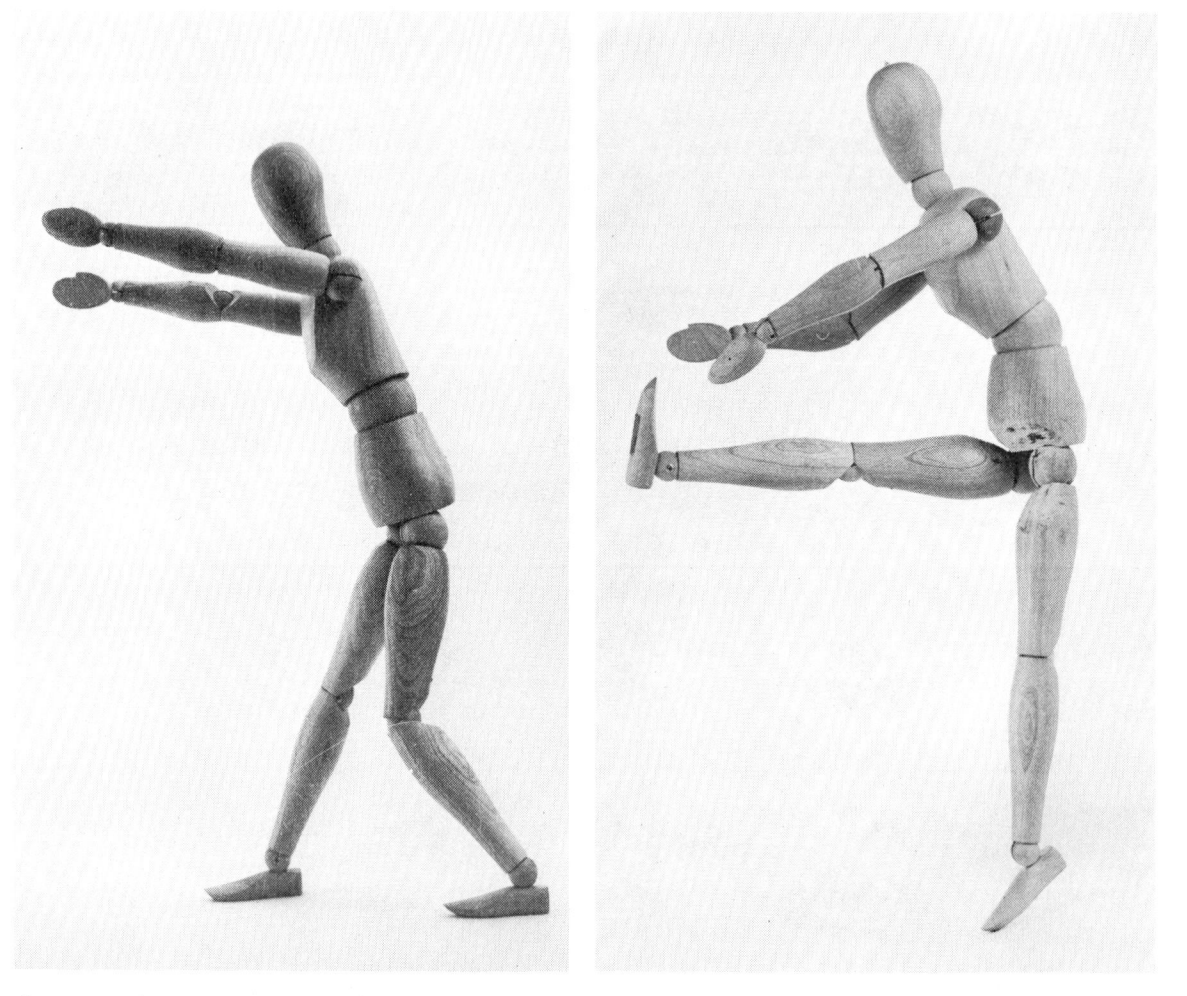

Figure 24. This exercise is a true kicking motion with the leg extended as high toward the head as possible in the follow-through.

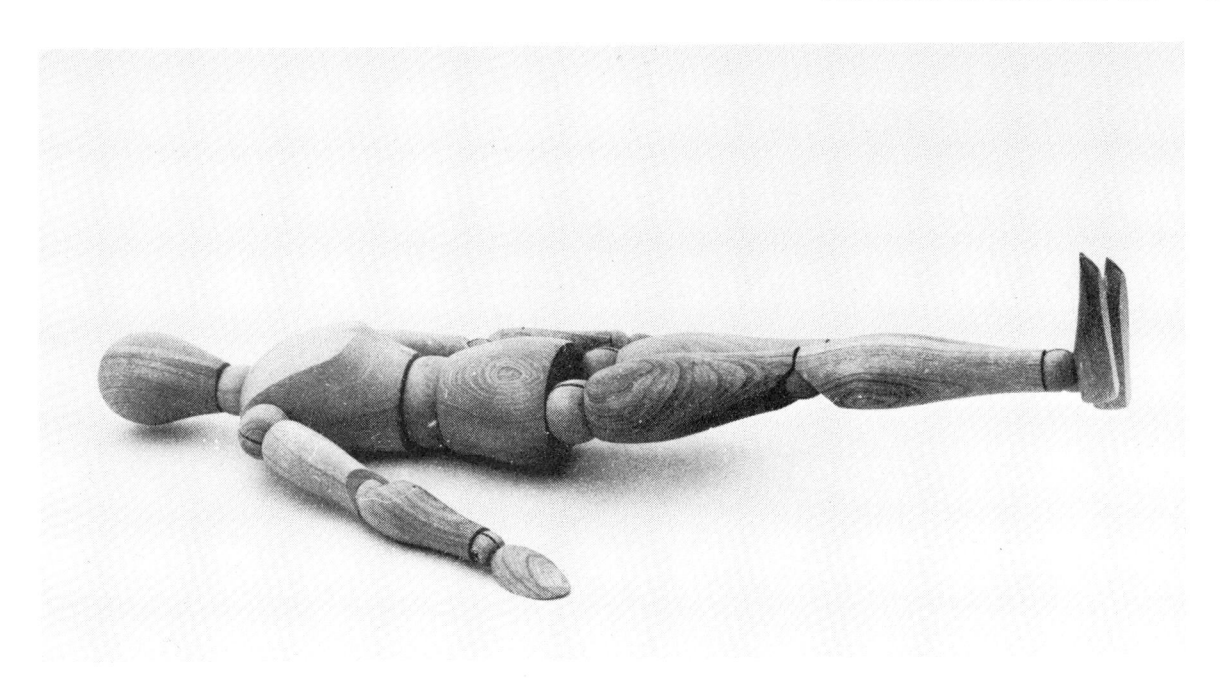

Figure 25. Lie flat on back and lift legs from floor. Spread legs as far as possible to the sides and bring back together. This is done as long as strength allows.

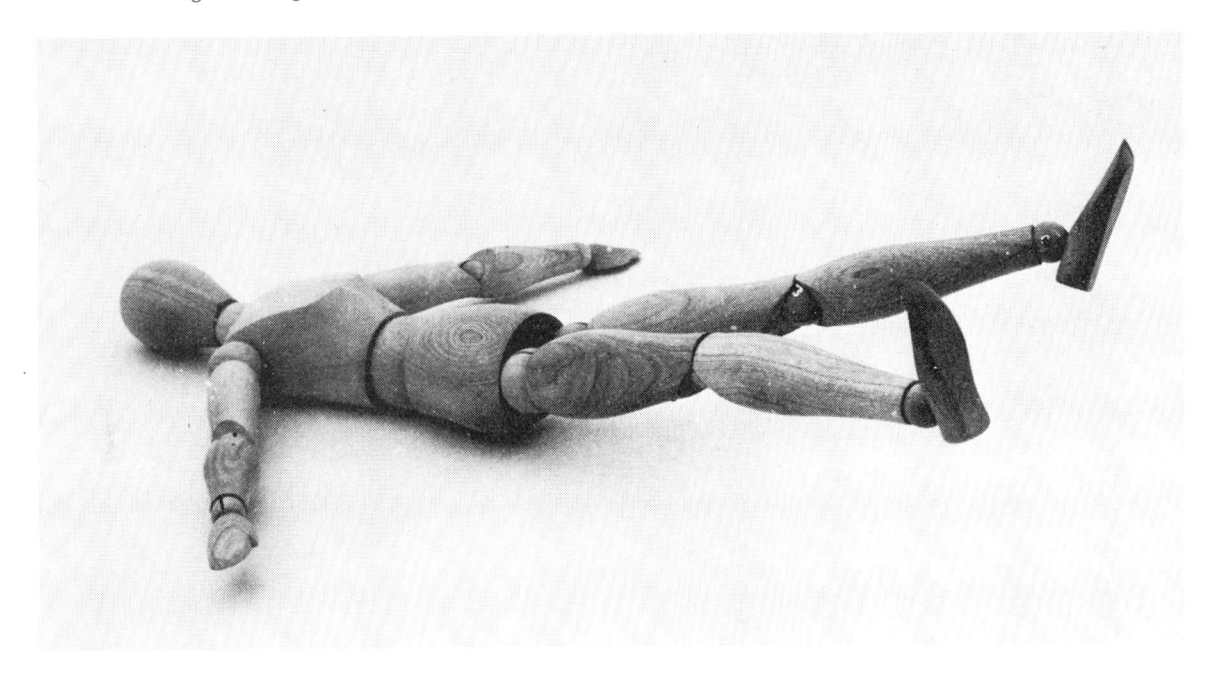

ing. This is a lateral stretch, one leg out to the side. You lean away from it while standing. The hurdler's stretch and the sprinter's start are helpful here too, as are the lotus squat and the forward squat.

The gluteal area

This is the place on which you sit. A gluteal pull is funny to everyone except the person who has it. It is very painful. We can protect against it with the isometric pucker, contracting all the area tightly. We also use the "seat roll," sitting and tightening the gluteal muscles, and the woodchopper (See figure 15), and the punter's kick, doing the latter as high as you can.

9
Hold that aching back

Here we have a collection of the strongest muscles in the body. The absolute maximum force put out by the body is with the long muscles in the back.

Because of the extreme strength and because it is one of the few areas where paired muscles oppose each other, any imbalance is immediately greatly magnified. The back responds to stresses elsewhere in the body. If you are favoring one leg, it is only a matter of time until this is transmitted to the back because of its overreaction. You get pains on one side or the other.

The principal function of the back is to move the trunk in various directions. It supports a vast amount of weight when it is holding the spine erect. Bend over and stand up. Just lifting the upper body places a strong stress on your back muscles.

Low back strain hits people of all ages, athletes and nonathletes. It comes from the overuse of the long muscles of the back. The low back has a joint between the spine and the pelvis which is particularly susceptible to strain. It doesn't have the bony support which the rib cage gives to the upper back, but is held together with ligaments.

Overuse will cause fatigue in those muscles. If one side becomes more fatigued than the other, the pull between them becomes terrific. One sign is that one leg becomes shorter than the other as one side of the pelvis is pulled up by the tight back muscles.

Among young athletes, unstable low back may be due to rapid growth. Boys suddenly shoot up, picking up a half-dozen inches in a year. The bone growth is so tremendous, the muscle strength can't keep up. The muscle mass doesn't develop fast enough to keep the back erect, and curvature of the spine and

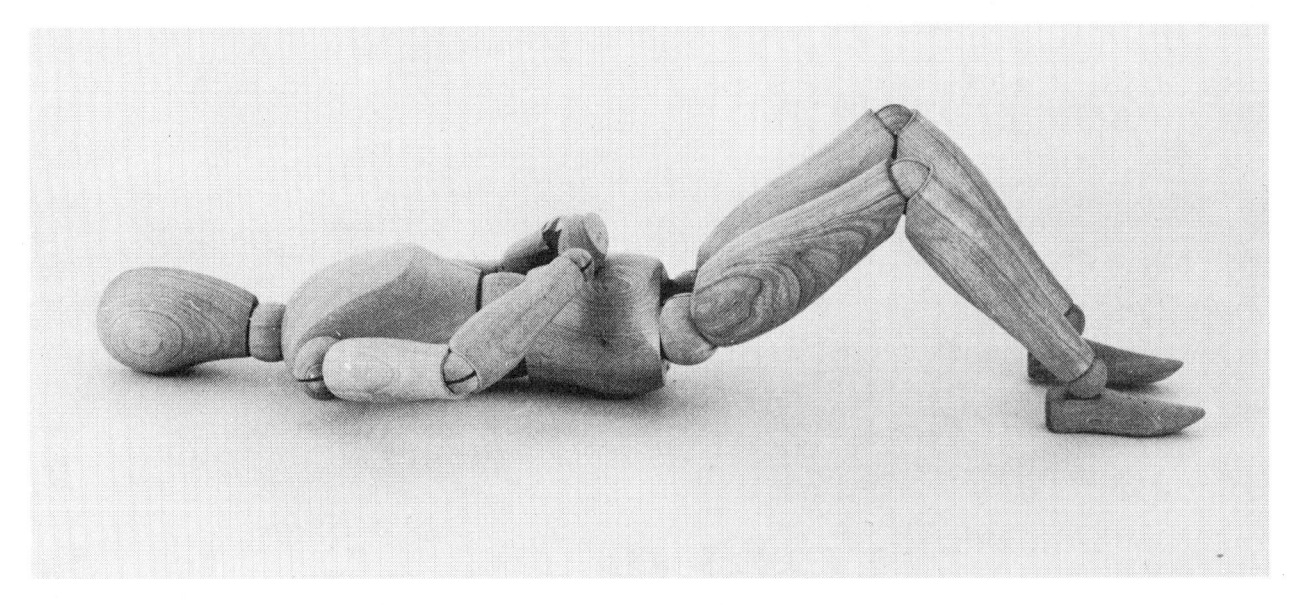

Figure 26. Lie on your back on the floor. Tighten the abdominal and seat muscles to roll the pelvis forward. Flatten the curve in the back fully against the floor and maintain.

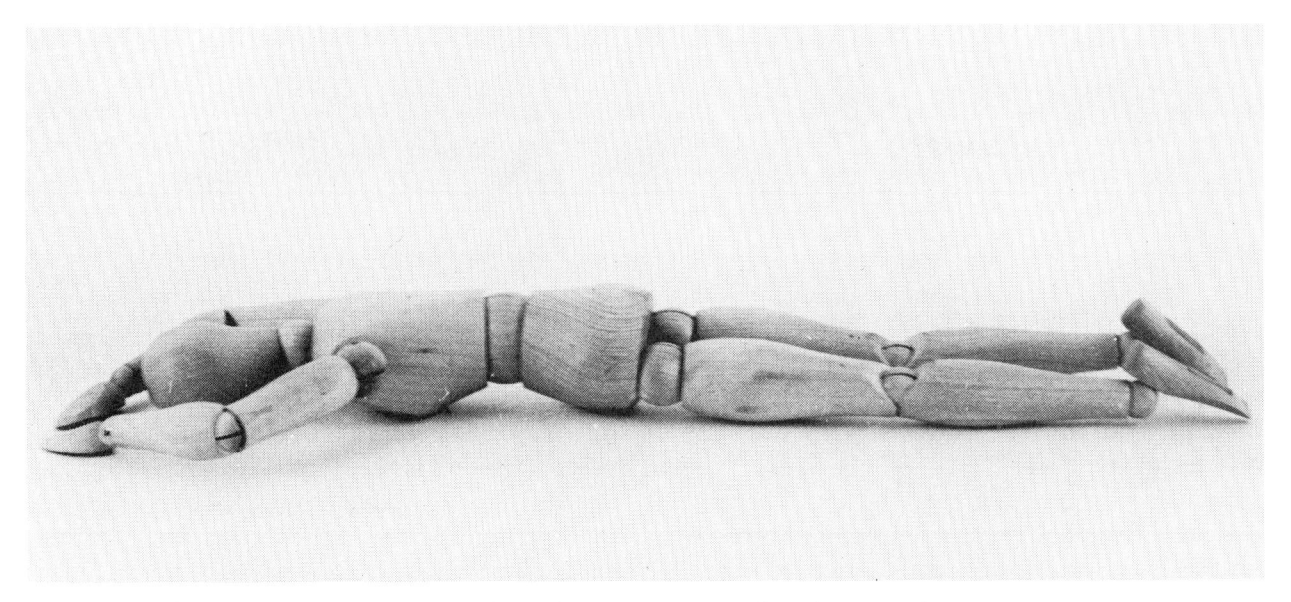

Figure 27. Isometric back exercise No. 2. This is the same exercise, done lying on the stomach. Tighten the muscles of the feet to drive the pelvis into the floor.

severe low backache may result. This is seen in the baseball catcher who can't get up and down or the basketball player who goes in to make a layup shot and can't get up to jump.

Then there are the muscle pulls and tears, due to sudden violent motion like a slip or a twist, or lifting with a sudden exertion.

The idea is to strengthen the long muscles and make an effort to equalize them. Stretching the back is important because the short muscles tend toward low back strain. Hamstring stretching should constitute about half your efforts in this connection. Sometimes a back problem will be relieved by hamstring stretching and nothing else.

In the strengthening exercises for the

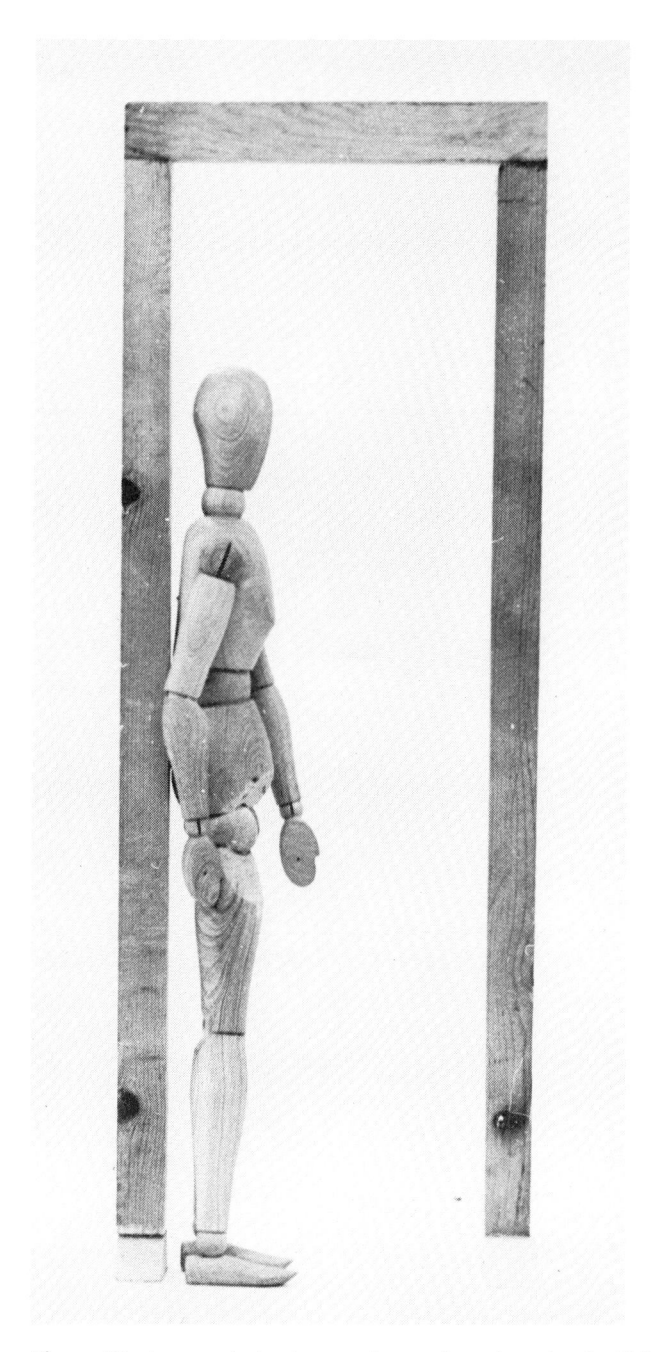

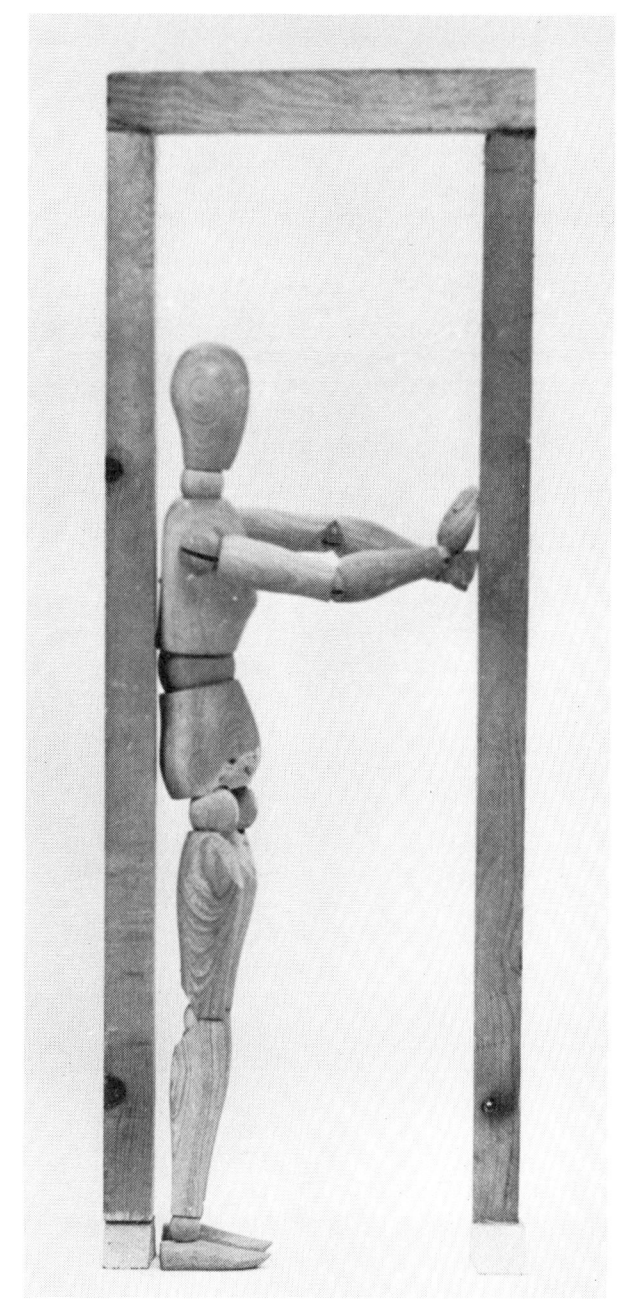

Figure 28. Isometric back exercise against door jamb. This is a similar exercise using leverage against the opposite side of the door jamb to flatten the back against the jamb.

back we do three isometrics. First, we lie flat on the floor and roll the pelvis forward. This is done by tightening the seat and abdominal muscles. Then, an attempt is made to get the small (arch) of the back to touch the floor.

Then, we do the same exercises, except we are lying on our stomachs.

Now, it's up on your feet. Stand in the doorway, your back against the jamb. Brace hands against the opposite side of the doorway, the gluteal area against the doorway also. You are trying to get your entire back to touch the doorway on the opposite side.

Stretching exercises are also essential for the back. Here are four important ones.

First is the knee-chest exercise in which you

40   **Conditioning for the high school athlete**

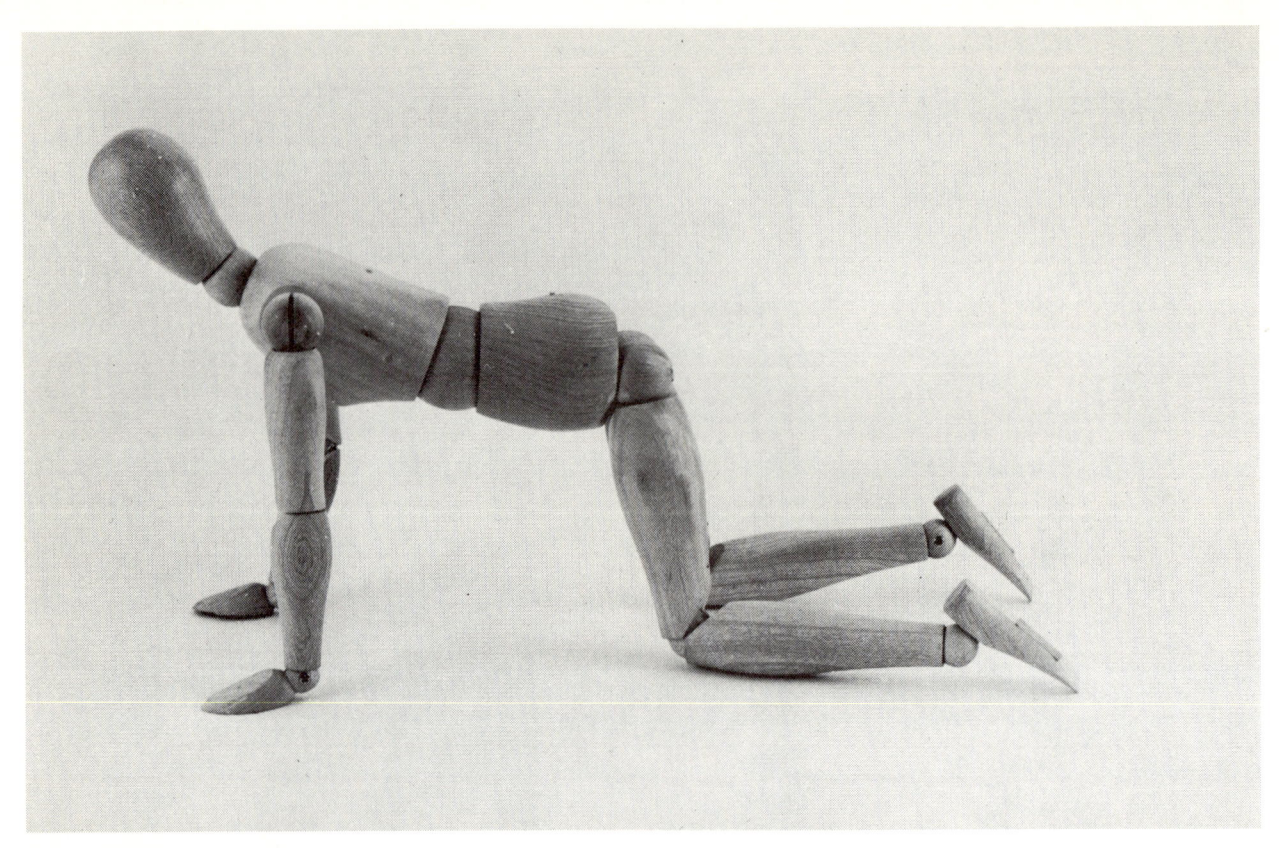

Figure 29. Back stretch. Fully arch the back and elevate the head. Then fully flex or hump the back and lower the head. The stretch in each direction should be maintained for five seconds.

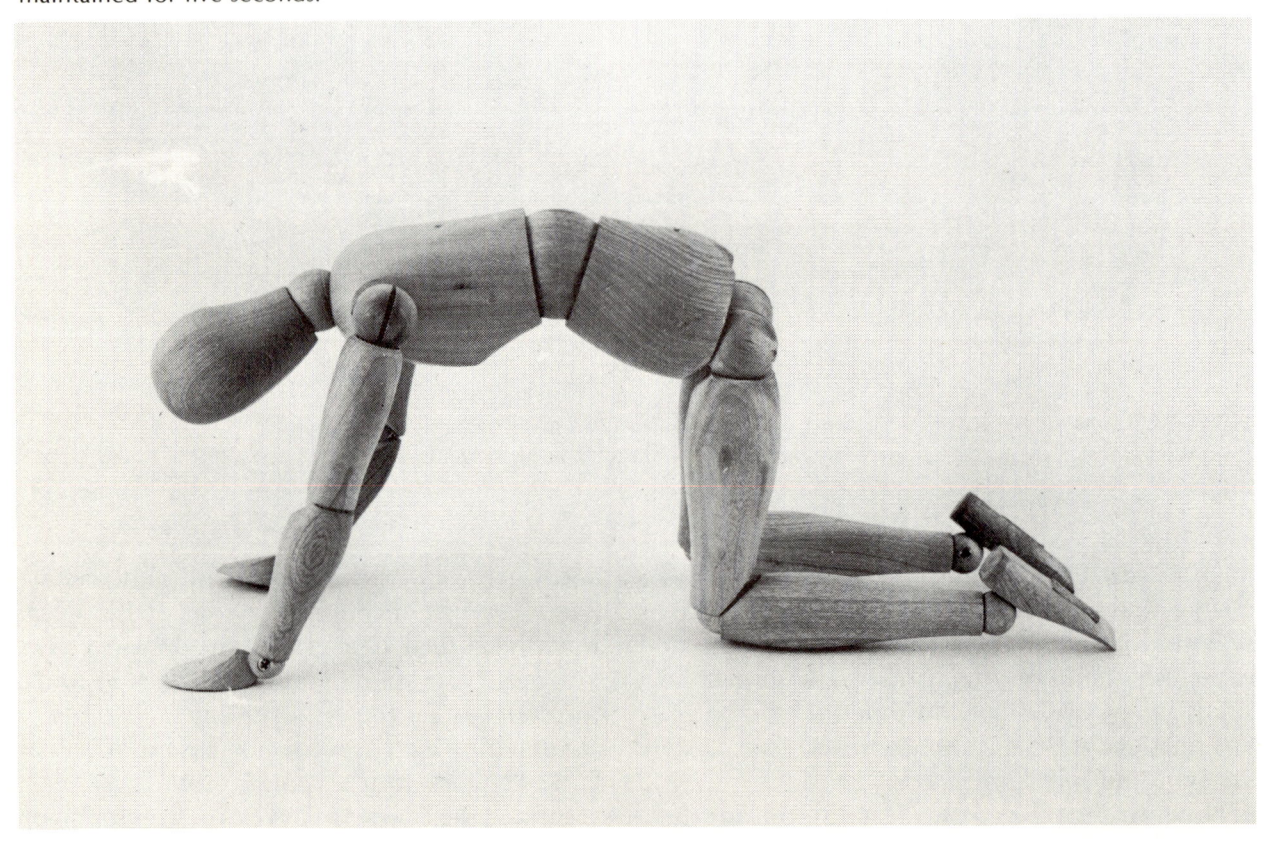

Hold that aching back 41

Figure 30. Grasp the knee from behind and bring forward toward the chest until a pulling in the lower back is felt. This exercise can be done with one knee at a time or with both legs simultaneously.

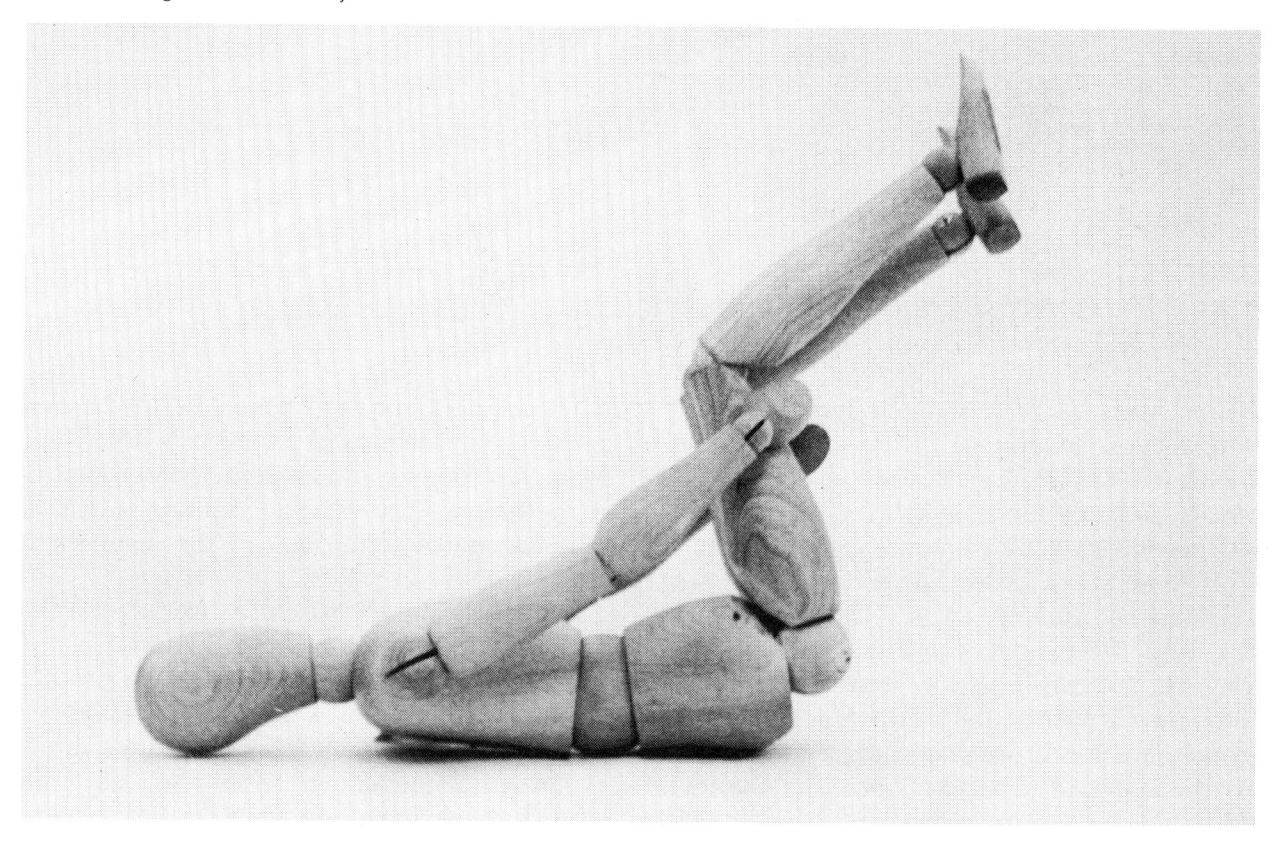

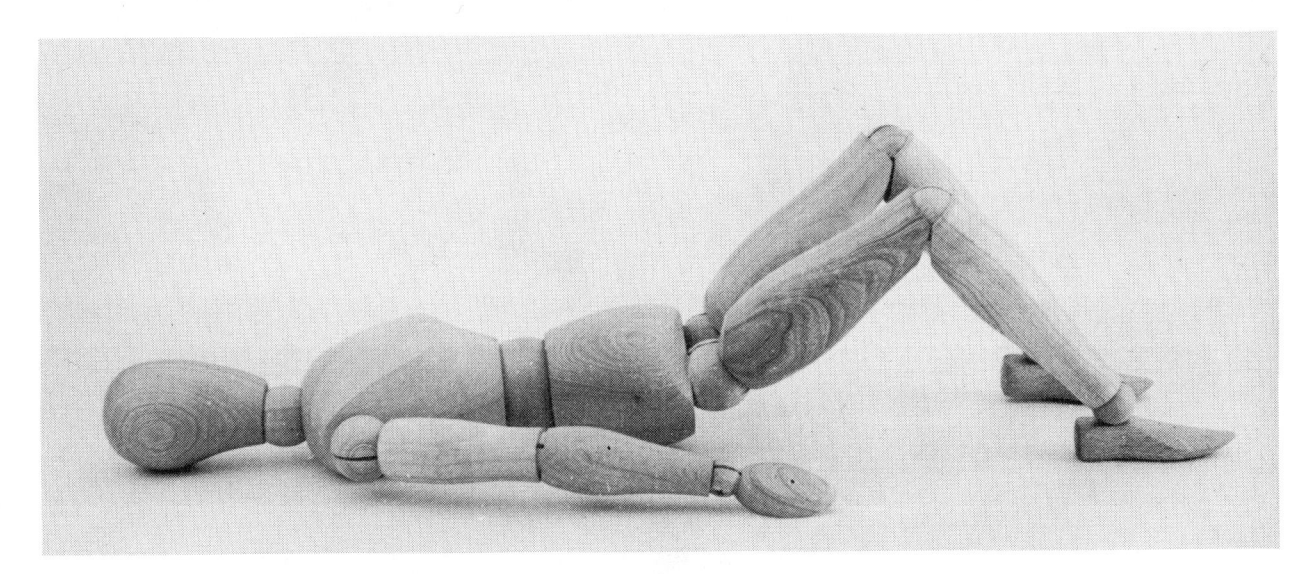

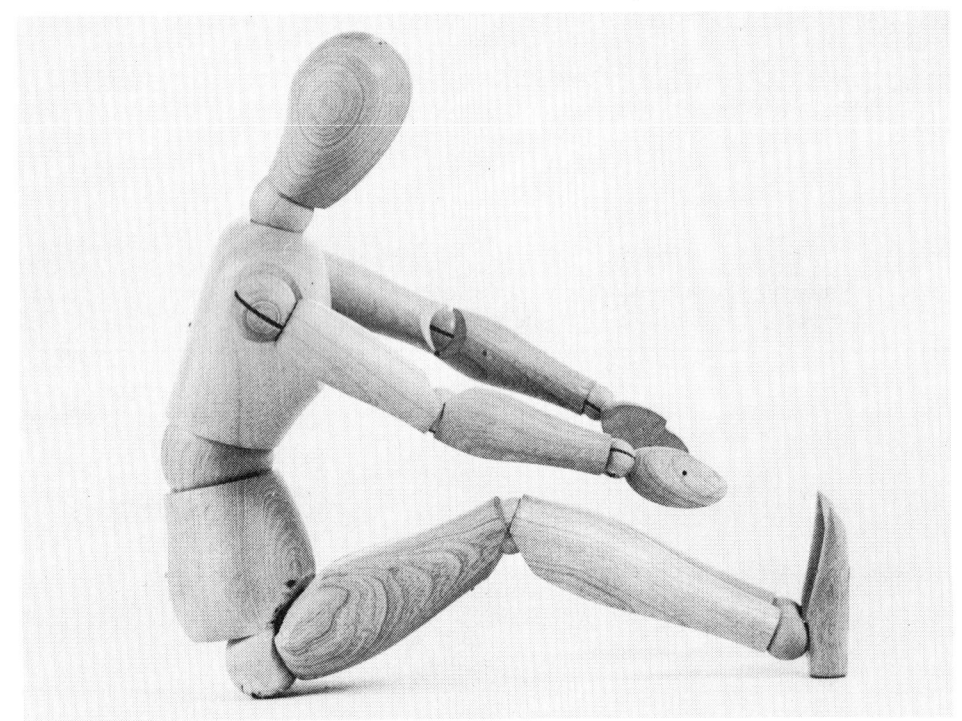

Figure 31. The sit-up is done with the knees bent.

lie on your back, clasp your hands around your bent knee, and pull it up to your chest. First each knee separately, then together; do it *slowly*, not in a rapid, jerky fashion.

Then there is the straight leg raising. Here it is done with locked knees, lying on your back. In addition, you can raise the leg with the knee flexed, and when you get it all the way up, you can begin to straighten the leg. This puts a pull on the hamstrings and back.

Next are the sit-ups. These can be done both by the standard method of touching the toes when you come up, and by touching the elbows to the opposite knees. On the second exercise, your hands are locked behind your head. This gives you both stretch and rotation, strengthening both the abdominal and back muscles, and it is the best of the sit-up exercises.

Finally, we have a flexibility exercise for the back. This one is done on all fours. In one motion, the back is arched, and the head is brought up as high as possible. From there, bow the back completely with the neck down as far as possible. There should be maximum effort in both directions.

Hold that aching back 43

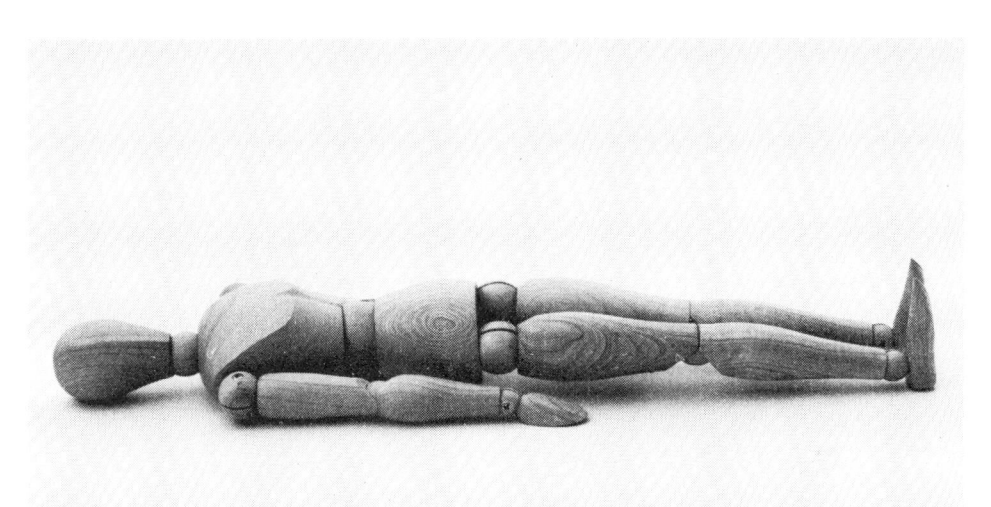

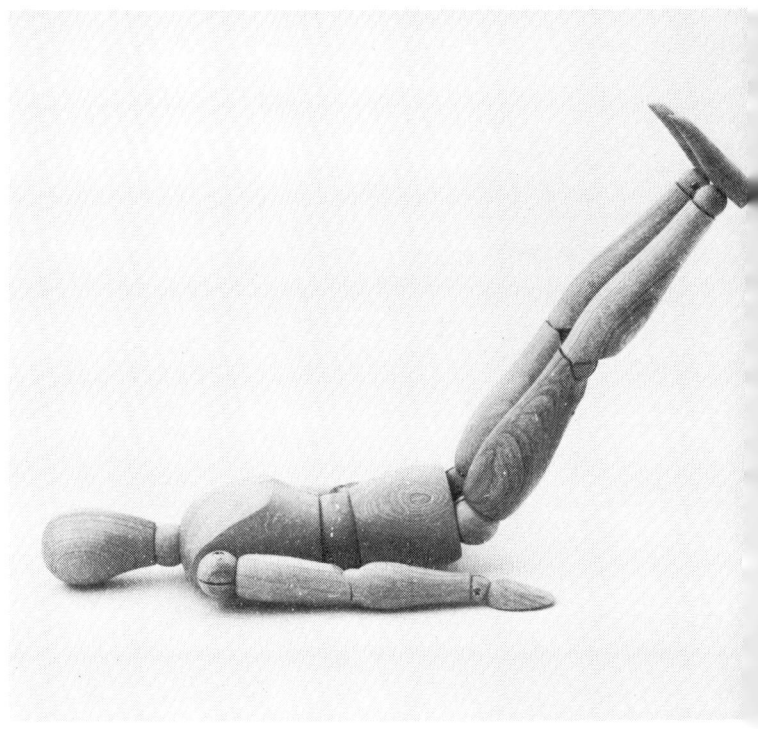

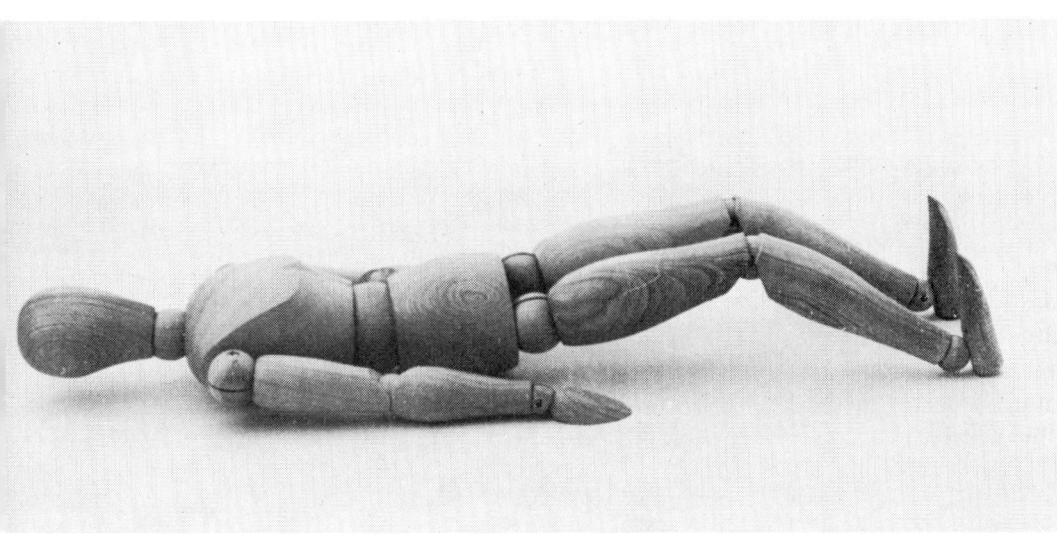

Figure 32. Straight leg raising. Lie on the back. Lift legs to 90 degrees and then slowly bring back down with stops.

10
It's what's up front that counts

The abdomen

The abdominal muscles, at the front of the trunk, are very strong but are subject to two problems. The muscles in the lower area are subject to pulls and tears and, once this happens, they are very slow to heal. It is a difficult area to treat. There is no taping possible, and supportive measures are practically nil. Weak abdominal muscles will cause a person to sustain trauma to his internal organs.

Hernia is a disabling injury to the abdomen. It is a rupture of the intestines through the lower abdominal wall. Under strong pressure it is possible to tear the wall and force the intestines through the fiber. The amount of force necessary varies from person to person, and the strength of the muscles in the inguinal (crotch) area is a factor. Hernia is nothing to fool with and medical advice is necessary here without delay. It isn't as though you're trying to play with a hamstring pull or a bruised calf. We are talking about serious injuries here, and as a preventive measure, efforts should be made to build up the abdominal muscles in young athletes.

There are two exercises, both done lying on the ground, which are beneficial. Sit-ups are particularly valuable for the upper abdominal muscles. Leg lifts have the same value for the lower abdomen.

On leg lifts, you lift your legs, move them apart, hold them at 50 degrees, return together, then continue toward the ground, making stops.

A good isometric exercise is the waist cincher. You merely pull in your abdomen as though you were attempting to touch your spine. Hold it for ten seconds. Do this three or

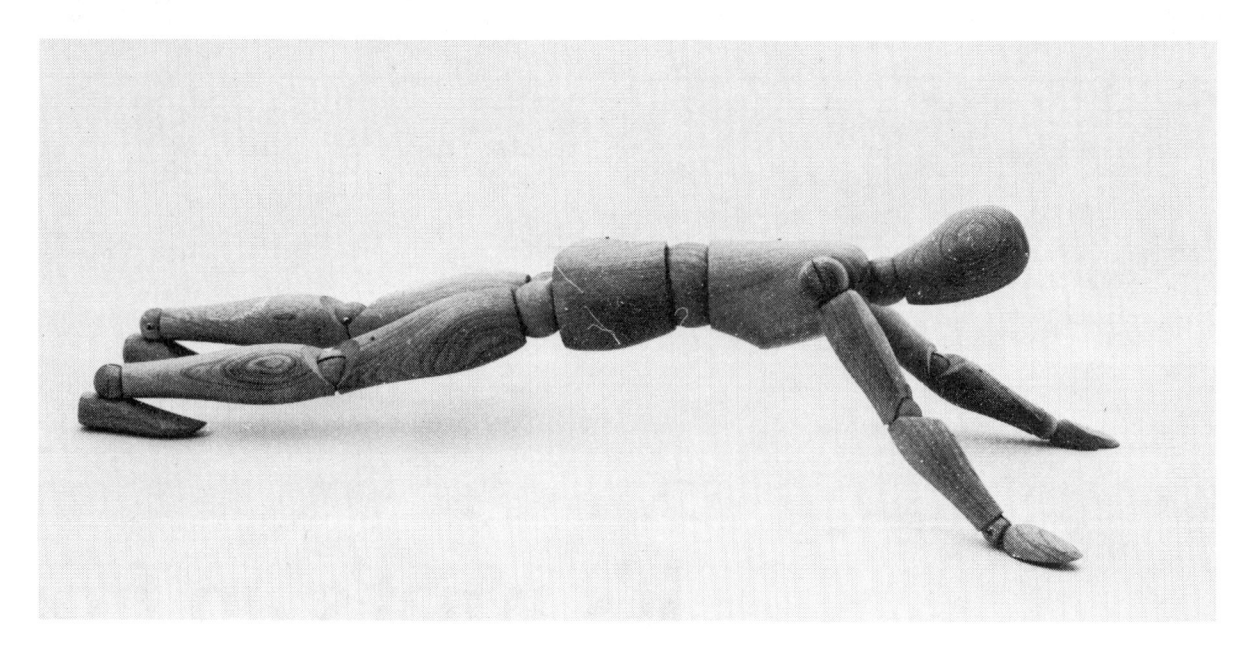

Figure 33. Start from a push-up position. Transfer weight to one arm and then roll the trunk so that the other arm is up.

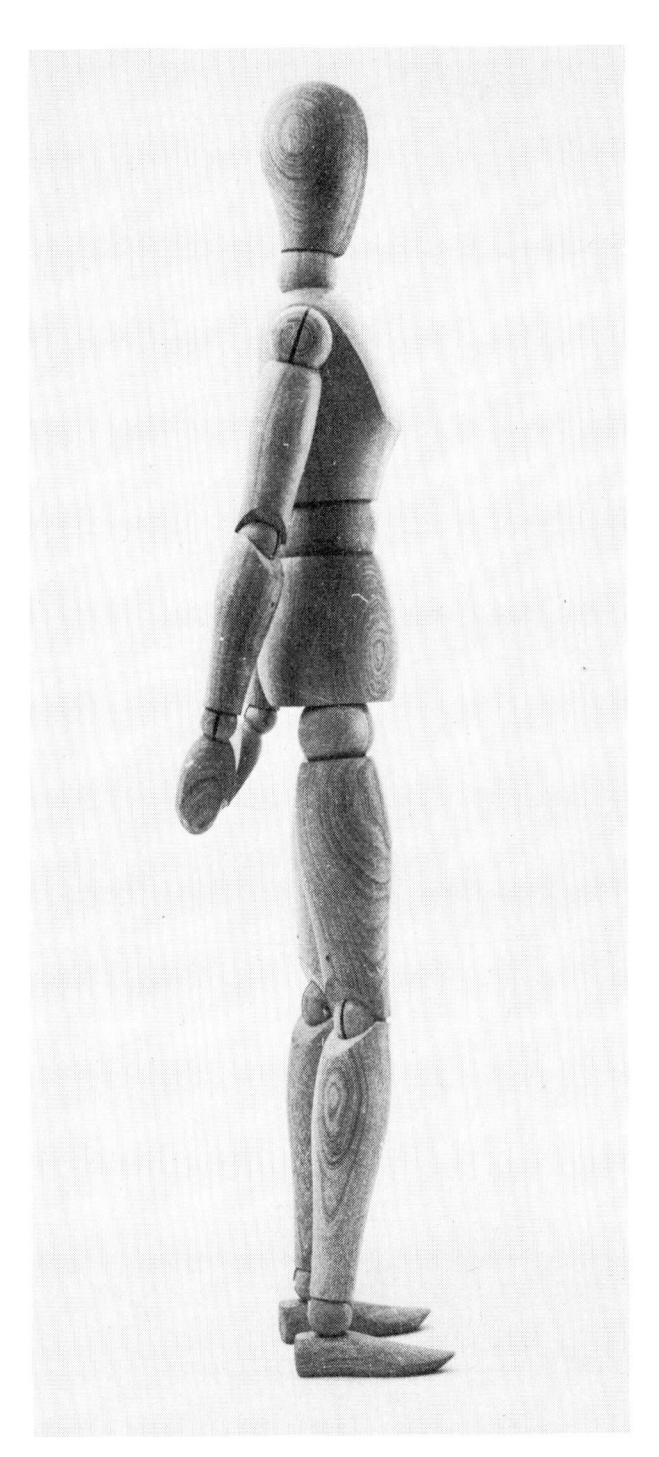

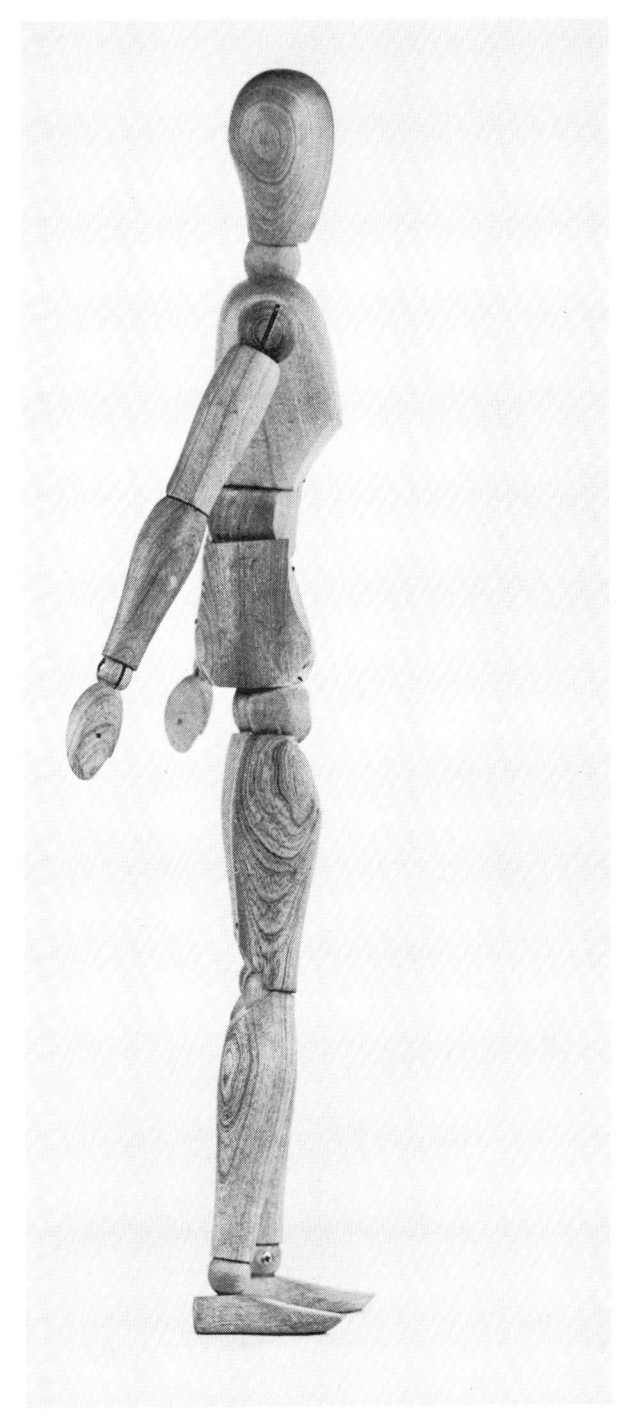

Figure 34. Pull in the abdominal muscles and attempt to touch them to the spine in the back. Hold for ten seconds.

four times a day, standing, spread throughout the day. It will not only add rapidly to the strength of your abdominal muscles, but it will help cut down on the waistline.

The medicine ball might seem a little old-fashioned but it has strong value, not only thrown back and forth, but also when it is rolled across the abdomen. When it is thrown directly at the abdomen you have no choice but to use those muscles there.

Stretching exercises for the abdomen are valuable, and the best is the "dog stretch" in the pushup position. You do exactly what you see a dog do when he sticks his hind legs out and stretches, arching his back. It will really stretch your abdominal muscles.

11
Take a deep breath

The chest

The chest is the area on top of the abdomen. Not too many chest injuries are disabling but the basic problem here is the lateral chest-wall pull. When you get one of these, you are inhibited in your movements because you can't breathe comfortably. The intercostal muscles connecting the ribs are affected; they are the ones that cause the chest to expand.

Weight training is best for these chest muscles. In isometric work you push your hands against each other in front of the chest.

Other exercises include sitting and standing windmills in which you rotate your arms in opposite directions. There is also the jumping jack—you raise your arms over your head, and in doing this you're pulling on the lateral chest muscles. There is also the lateral stretch with weights. You hold a 10- to 20-pound dumbbell, and bend all the way over to the side with the weight on your lower arm.

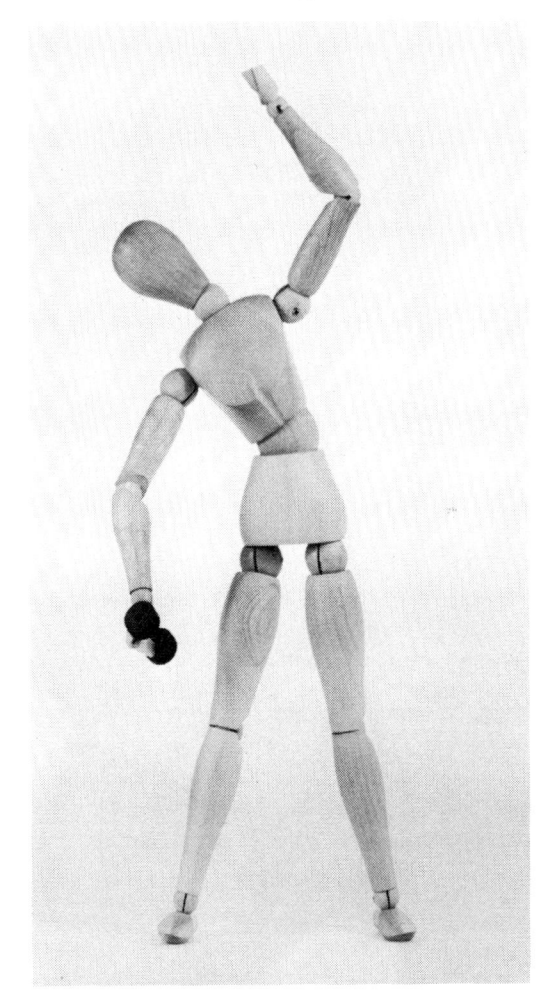

Figure 35. Hold a ten-pound weight in one hand. Bend the trunk to the side of the weight and raise the other arm until stretching is felt in the chest wall.

12
The big reach

Upper extremities

Like the knee, the shoulder is a joint doing a job in athletics for which it was *not* intended. Hence, it is prone to injury. It is further abused because its strength is not in the direction in which we use it. The shoulder would be at its strongest if we walked on all fours. It is held together by rotator cuff muscles, of which more later.

Among the injuries to which the shoulder is subject is subluxation. This is something not quite as severe as dislocation. The shoulder slides partially out of the socket and slides back in by itself.

The shoulder socket is very, very shallow and, if the rotator cuff muscles are not strong, the shoulder simply will pop out under strong pressure. As it does this it stretches the ligamentous structure and as it comes out it knocks off the edge of the structure forming the socket, making it even shallower and more subject to popping out again.

As this goes on, the shoulder will keep going, until finally it will go right over the edge of the socket and will be completely dislocated.

This is very painful and debilitating. It then must be manually replaced by a medical person. With each dislocation it becomes easier to dislocate and relocate, and you actually have people who can pop their shoulder back by themselves.

The injury comes with sudden violent force against the structure of the capsule and the cuff tears and pulls. A good example here is the arm tackle in football. A boy sticks his arm out and someone runs right through it. The injury causes bleeding, pain, and swelling in

52 **Conditioning for the high school athlete**

Figure 36. Standard push-up exercise.

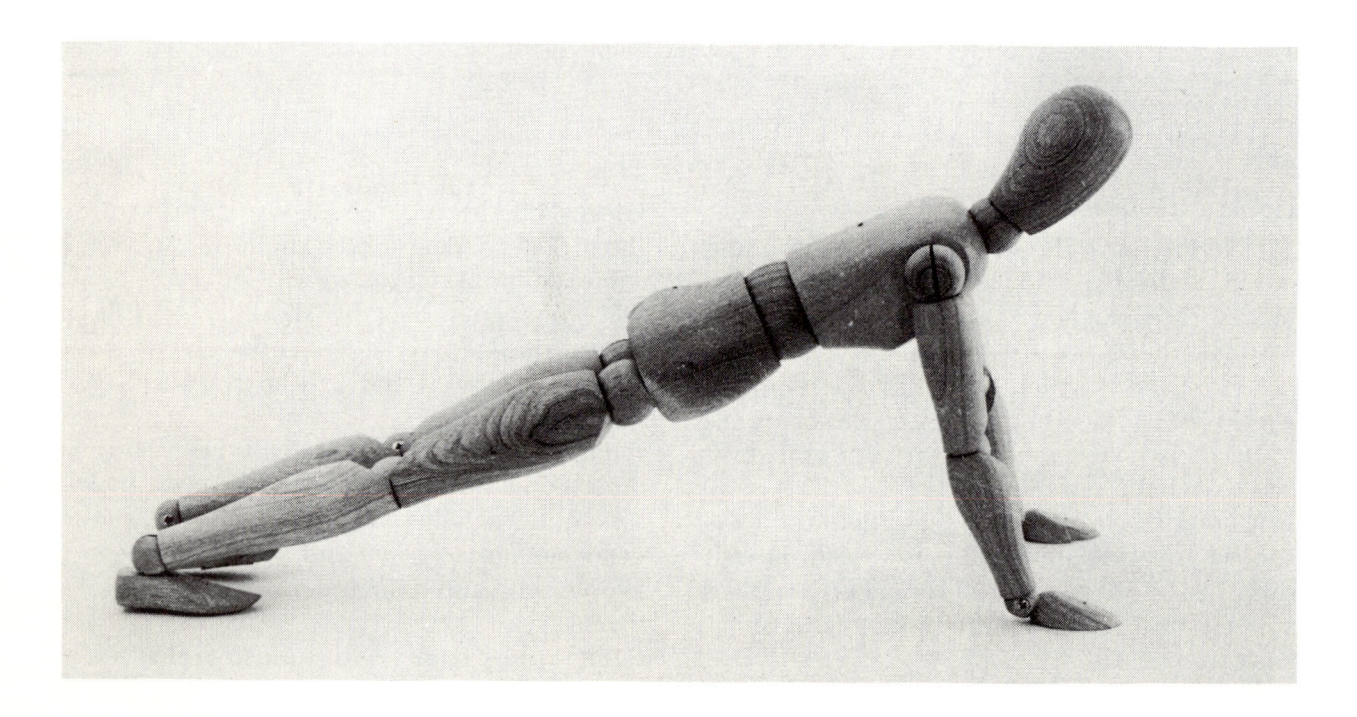

The big reach 53

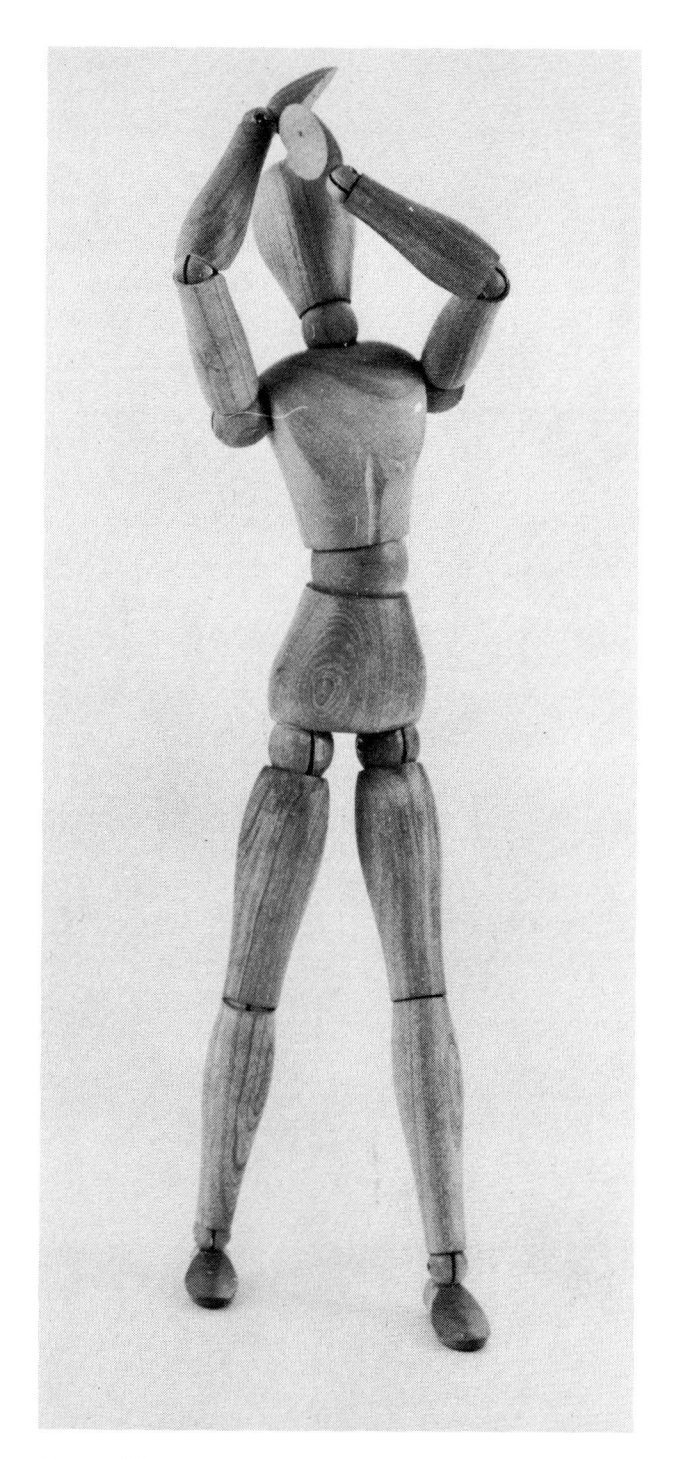

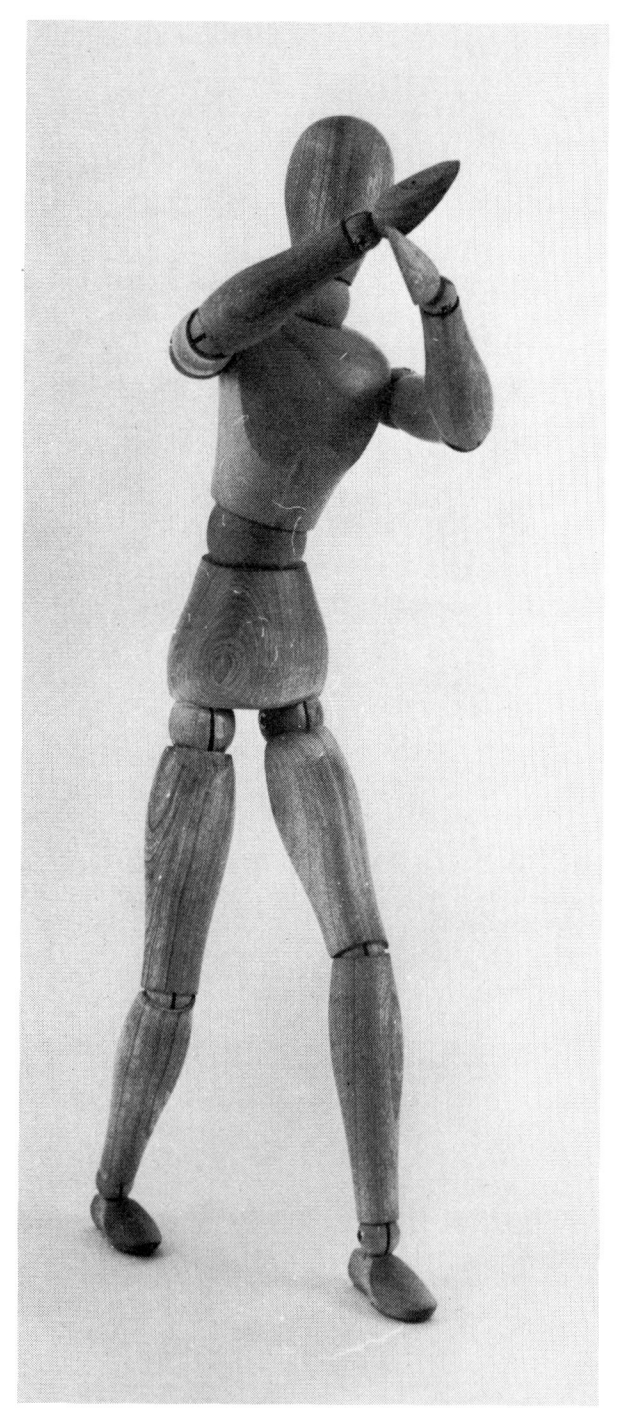

Figure 37. Isometric passing exercise against resistance. The passing arm is brought through a normal passing motion while being resisted in its effort by the opposite arm. Arms are then reversed.

the muscle and inability to use the shoulder or move the arm. Other violent motions, like a diver hitting the water badly, can also cause this injury.

Another shoulder injury is tendinitis of the head of the biceps. This is common among baseball players, and when severe, a pitcher can't throw.

Figure 38. Push-ups from chair. Do basic push-up maneuver while balanced between three chairs. This allows the body to go lower than the level of the hands at the downpoint of the pushoff.

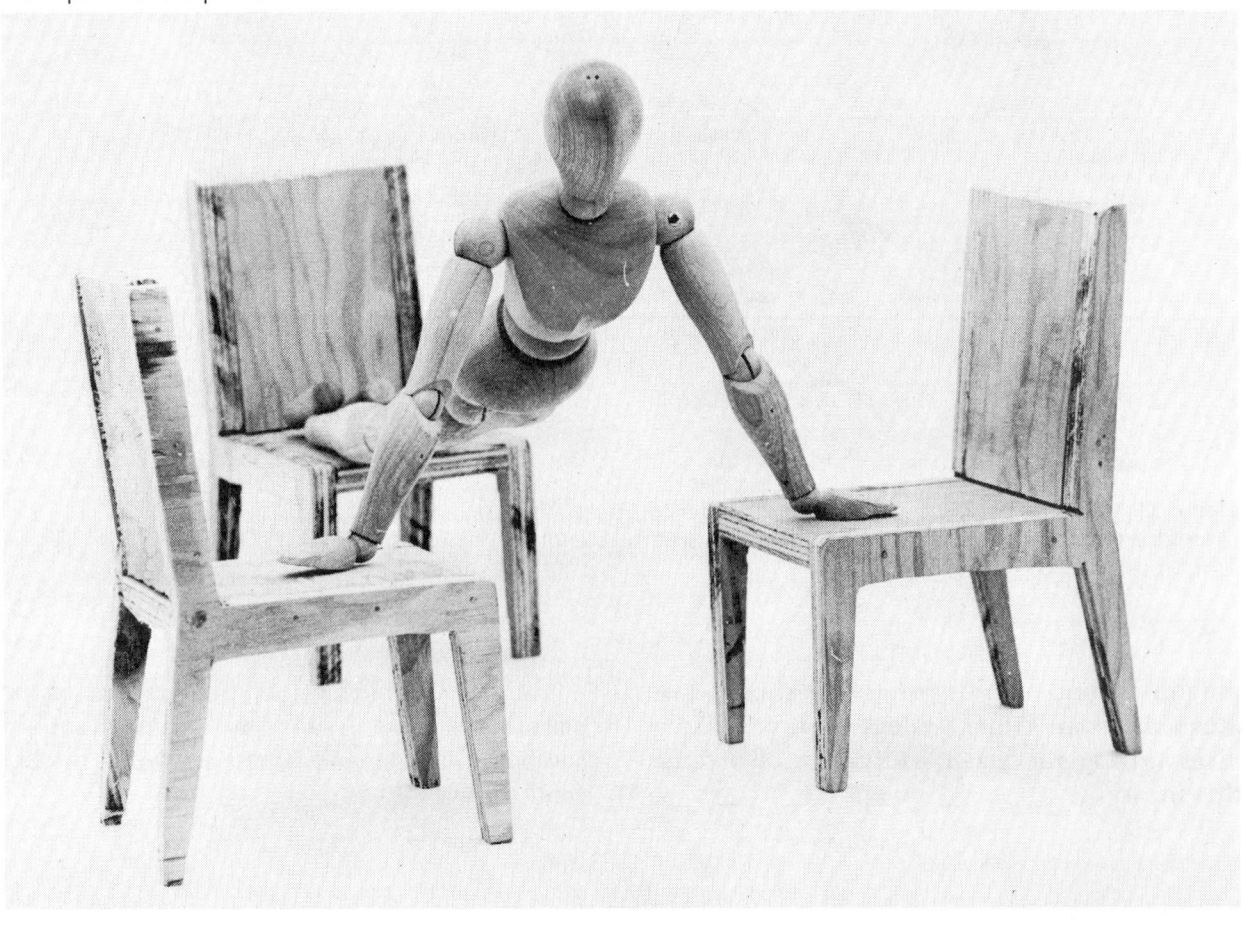

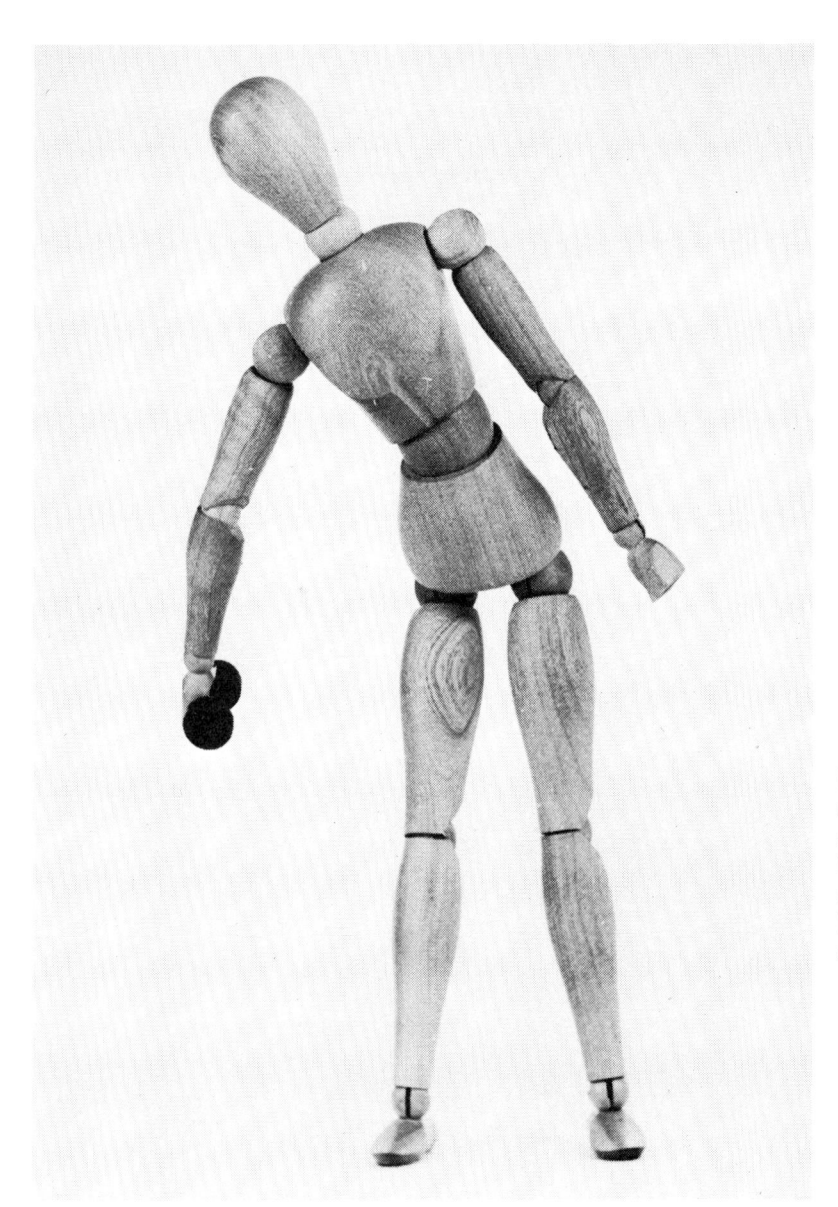

Figure 39. Pendulum. Hold five-pound dumbbell in one hand. Keep the shoulders completely relaxed. Bend the body to the side of the dumbbell hand, and rotate until the dumbbell swings like a pendulum. Perform revolutions in each direction.

There are exercises for strengthening shoulder muscles. Isometric passing is one. Here you attempt to go through the passing motion without the football, bringing your arm through an arc and putting opposite resistance on it with the other arm.

There are isometrics with a basketball. This is the same type of effort we talked about in the groin pull. The ball is held and squeezed close to the chest, halfway in, and extended.

Using the friendly doorway again, there are isometrics in which you brace on one side, push on the other. The positions are varied here so you're changing the angle.

Pushups, the standard variety and others, are helpful. The "others" include pushups using three chairs. You drop your body all the way down between the chairs. It's a tough one but a great builder.

Stretching is important, and this can be accomplished by hanging by the arm. Chinning is an excellent exercise and is one of the oldest in the world. Do it both ways, palms facing away from you and palms facing toward you.

The pendulum exercise is extremely effective and is easy to set up. You need a 5- or 10-pound dumbbell or a can of paint with the lid

Figure 40. Support the body by one arm from a chinning bar. When you feel fatigued, change to the other arm.

clamped down tight. The body is flexed to the side. The entire arm is limp, the hand holding the dumbbell or the can. You then rotate your body until you can get that weight swinging in a circle like a pendulum. It pulls those relaxed muscles and stretches them in the shoulder. It is most important that the shoulder muscles be completely relaxed and that the dumbbell not be pushed around in a circle. The dumbbell must be allowed to circle by centrifugal force in order to accomplish its purpose.

The big reach 57

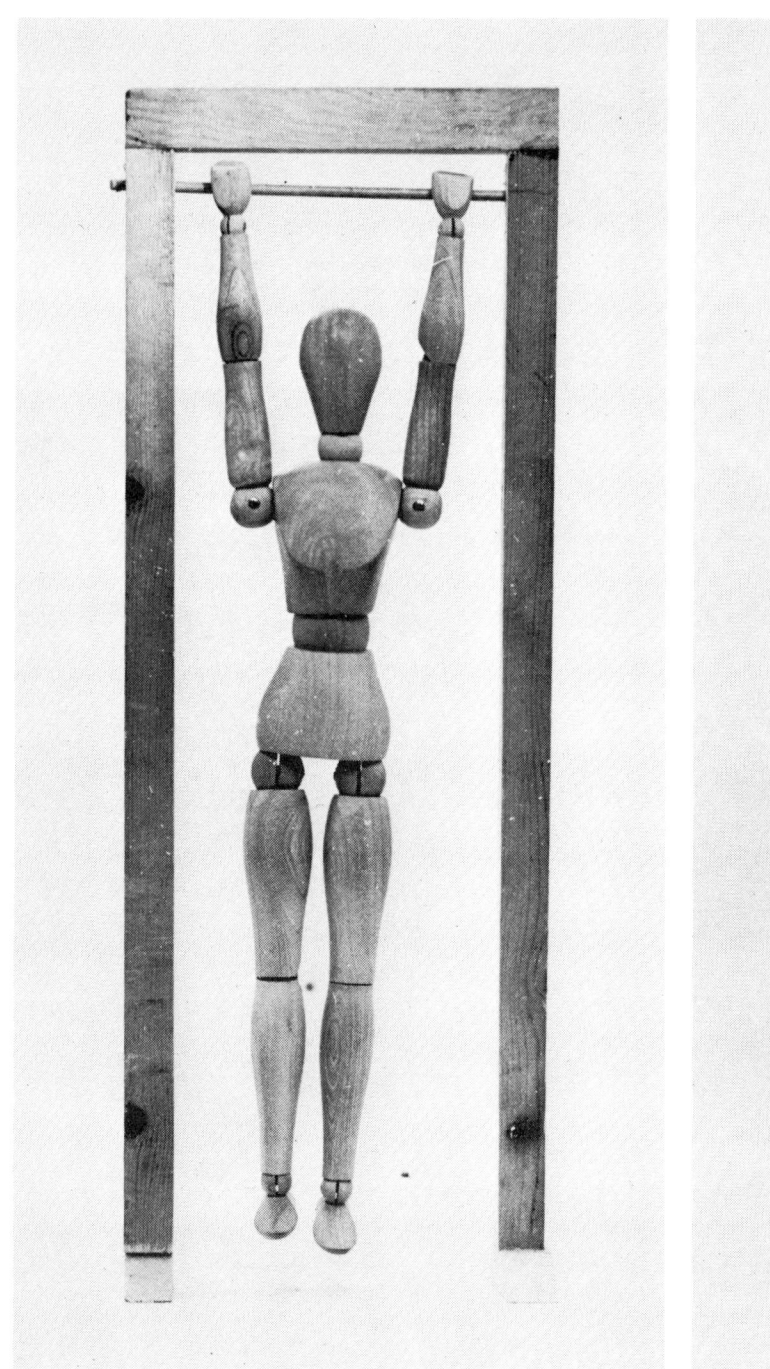

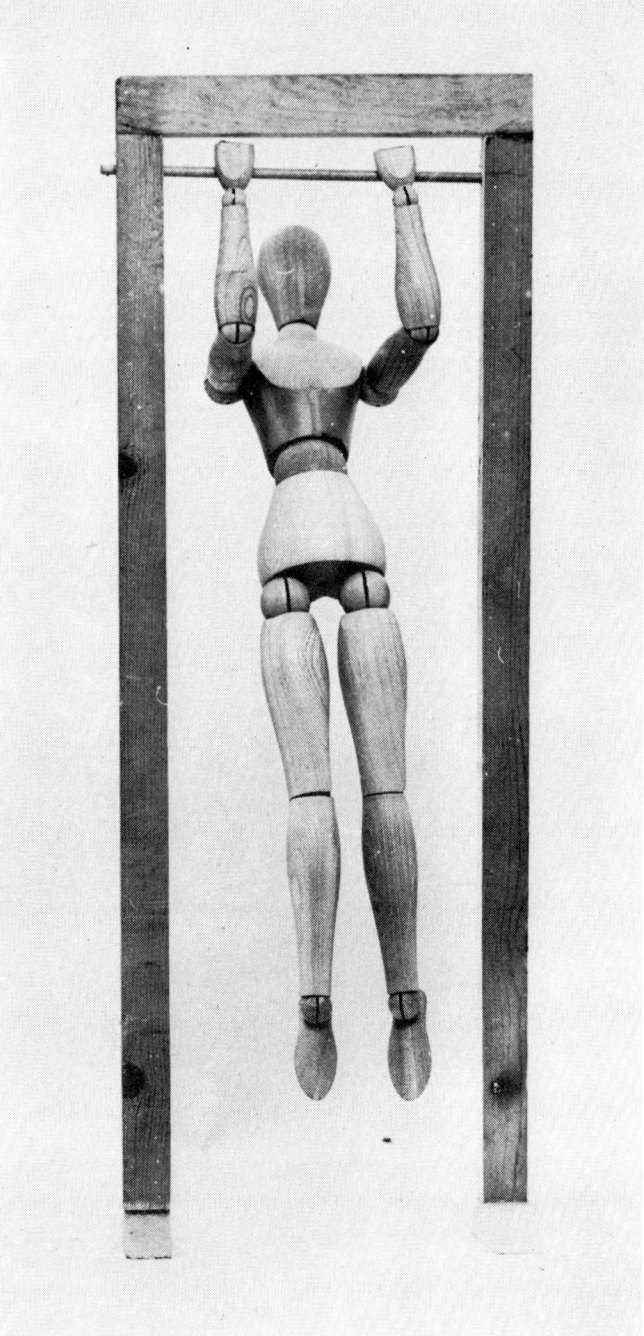

Figure 41. Standard chin-ups from a chinning bar should be done both with the palms facing away from you and facing toward you.

13
On the cuff

The wrist

The wrist, a small part of the body, is relatively out in the open and subject to injury by hyperextension, forward or backward. This is easily the wrist's biggest problem.

Here, stretching is of no value, so we stay away from it. But we do have a couple of tested recipes for strengthening the area.

One is isometric, and it uses the rubber-ball squeeze, an old trick. The other, and best because it helps not only the wrists but the forearms and even the shoulders, is the exercise using a can of paint filled with cement, tied with a piece of clothesline and attached to a broomstick piece two feet long. You hold this contraption at arms length and try to wind it (roll it up) onto the stick. You roll with one hand, grab the stick with the other, and alternate. If you can't get cement, fill the can with wet sand or anything that will give you a heavy weight with which to work.

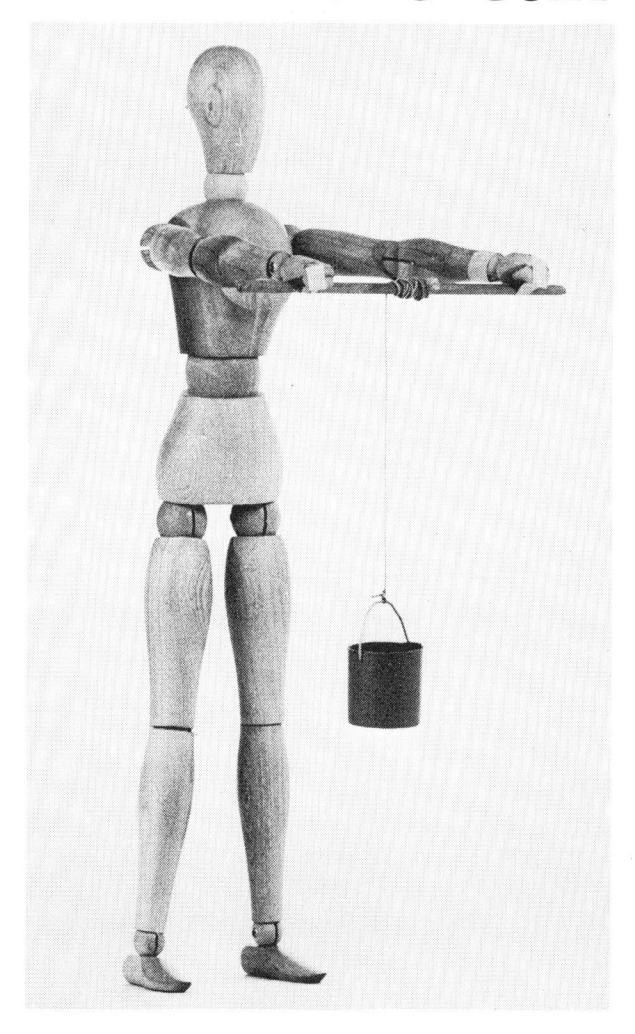

Figure 42. Attach a weight to a length of cord. Then tie the cord to a broomstick so the weighted cord can be rolled up both clockwise and counterclockwise to strengthen the wrists.

14
Proceed with caution

The neck

Neck injuries are probably the most serious faced by an athlete, and the subject is easily the most important in this book. It's axiomatic in sports conditioning and medicine that a knee injury can end a career, but a *neck* injury can end a life, or leave the unfortunate recipient a paraplegic, doomed to wheelchair existence or worse.

There are three injuries to which the neck is susceptible, depending on the direction the neck is moved, laterally, left or right, up or down.

First, there is hyperextension or "whiplash." This comes when the head snaps back too hard, but it will usually *not* cause a broken neck. The pain in the neck muscles is rather severe as a result but the muscle support is ample enough to prevent disaster.

Then, there is lateral hyperflexion or overstretch, and nerve injury can result from this. The nerves that supply the arm and shoulder come out of the back side of the cervical spine. If stretched too far the nerves can be pulled or torn. An injury here can sideline someone for six weeks or six months. If the nerves are torn there might be permanent paralysis of the arm, so it's a very serious situation.

Finally, there's hyperflexion, where the neck is forcibly flexed with the chin down on the chest. This is the injury that causes the broken necks, severing the spinal cord and causing paralysis.

Among young athletes, two problems are encountered—one a physical condition, the other a playing tactic. First, there's the too-long neck, which sounds funny unless you happen to have one. If a boy is so endowed, he risks injury in a contact sport unless his neck

62 Conditioning for the high school athlete

Figure 43. Neck bridges. These are done both facing up and down. The arm supports should be removed so the entire weight rests on the neck.

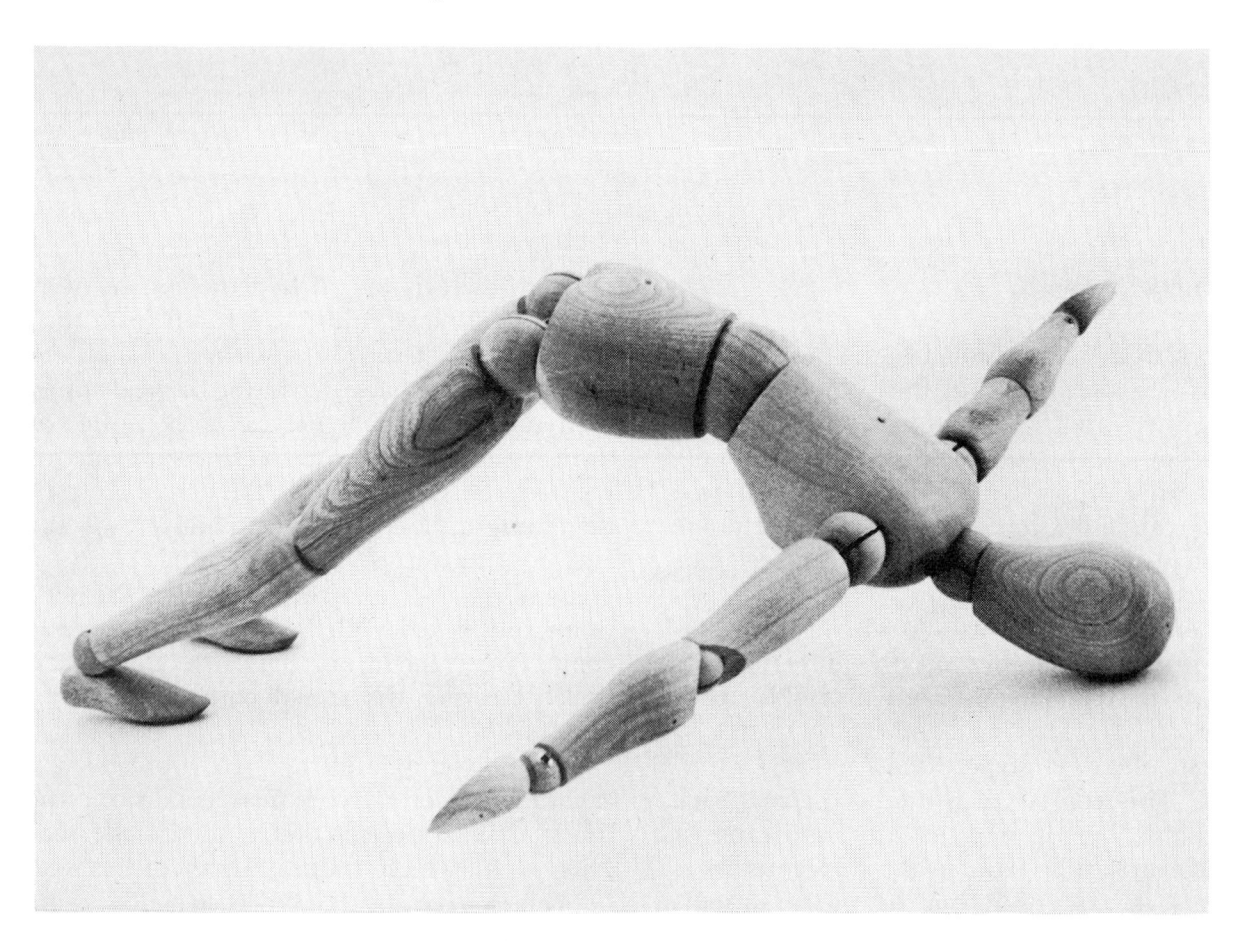

Figure 44. This can be done in all four directions against the resistance of a partner.

is artificially supported with a special collar. In the past, most of these have been poorly designed and haven't been worn properly.

We are starting to see new ones that fulfill their purpose. They are like an orthopedic collar in which you can turn your head and look up, but you cannot overstretch in any direction.

"Spearing" is the other problem. This is something which is fraught with danger for both the boy doing it and the boy getting it. Boys are taught to tackle headfirst into the opponent's breastbone. This is the "face mask in the numbers" type of tackling. Though spearing has been ruled illegal, the "face mask in the numbers" blocking and tackling is still practiced in many areas. The player won't hurt himself if he keeps his head up. If he, through fear, ducks his head, he risks hyperflexion.

If boys were taught to tackle with the shoulder to one side of the ball carrier we wouldn't see these injuries. No matter how much effort is devoted to strengthening the neck, hyperflexion is a problem because neck muscles aren't that strong.

To strengthen the neck there are exercises and isometrics. The neck bridge is effective but children between 8 and 12 shouldn't do it. In the exercise you get your rear end up and support yourself on your head and toes. You can also turn face down and do the same exercise.

Isometric exercises include placing your head against the wall and pushing, or having a partner push back against your head.

There is also a general group of appliances which work on a tension rope principle. You can set the tension to suit yourself. You put your head into the harness and work against the tension. It's like a set of weights, except that weights aren't used. These appliances can also be used to exercise other parts of the body; they cost between 15 and 20 dollars.

15
Getting it together

The head

Last stop on our anatomical tour is the head, where it all starts and finishes. A few thoughts are timely here.

First, certain sports call for headgear—football, baseball when batting, lacrosse, hockey. There's nothing clever or exciting about playing without your headgear if it's called for. And make certain that it fits, football helmets in particular. Face masks should be in good repair with no exposed surfaces.

If a boy is participating in boxing or wrestling he should wear the head protectors prescribed. In wrestling it may not look as daring as if you're not wearing such gear, but this is a pretty small return for a cauliflowered ear. The gear is mandatory in wrestling matches. In practice, the foolhardy business of not wearing the head protectors is to be severely condemned. A cauliflower injury can be picked up just as easily here as in a match.

One head injury that is of prime importance is the type received when a player is knocked out or knocked groggy. Football has a very picturesque description for someone deprived of his normal ability to think because of a blow which has caused a concussion. They say "he's had his bell rung."

There's nothing funny about the phrase. A boy in this condition should be through for the afternoon, and any coach who sends him back in after "his head has cleared" is wrong.

A boy in this condition can sustain serious injury if he takes a similar blow within the time span of an hour or two.

The temptation to use a star player under these conditions is a strong one. Parents of boys playing under these conditions must take a firm stand—no further play unless the school guarantees, through its medical officer, that this practice has been stopped.

In addition to the player not being returned to the game just after his injury, it is imperative he not return to practice or contact until his symptoms are completely gone and he has had adequate time to recover. This is one injury that requires medical clearance before a return to practice is advisable.

16
What it's all about

Physical conditioning

Conditioning is simply taking the physical attributes of the body, matching them with the development that we have discussed earlier in the book, and attempting to bring them into some type of coordinated performance. Conditioning, obviously, is of extreme importance.

By increasing a youth's coordination, speed, and stamina, as well as sharpening his skills, we are searching for the top degree of performance of which he is capable. A good comparison is taking a raw lump of clay and shaping it into a bust or statue that is not only aesthetically pleasant to the eye but capable of giving great satisfaction to both the beholder and the creator.

Now that the athlete has done the body-building exercises, he must attempt to capitalize on them by getting the maximum value from them. This means taking a highly complex physical mechanism in its raw state—a young athlete not yet having reached maturity—and trying to organize it into some kind of productive unit.

In the age group we are discussing, the nervous system has not yet caught up with the physical development. Therefore, it becomes increasingly obvious that developing coordination is one of the most important parts of conditioning. The young athlete has great recuperative powers, natural instincts and drives toward success. However, many of these qualities haven't yet been fully developed. Conditioning helps to do just this.

Teaching new techniques

Many of the moves in athletics are unnatural, something that goes against the natural makeup of the body. Probably the most unnatural move of all is the golf swing. The natural tendency when you come down is to bend your elbow and push the club through with your right hand, your power hand if you are right-handed.

The natural swing is the baseball swing. With elbows bent, the wrists snap through but the power comes from your dominant hand. In golf, the left elbow is locked and you are pulling the club through with your left hand and merely steering it with your power hand.

Another unnatural movement is throwing a baseball, particularly for the pitcher on all pitches except an overhand fast ball. In the curve or the slider, there is rotation and snapping of the elbow, which is a completely unnatural motion and which must be taught. A sore arm is the body's way of protesting against doing something that wasn't on the original list.

In tennis, the natural thing to do is to swat at the ball as it comes at you but you are really supposed to hit the ball from behind you. The shot put in track and field is also a completely unnatural motion.

However, it is easy enough to teach young persons new techniques. The young person's body has not yet formed solid ideas of how things should be done. Again, we have the idea of the raw clay which can be molded in any of several ways.

Developing coordination, speed, stamina

In addition to teaching the body these unusual or unnatural movements, it is important as a part of conditioning to increase coordination, improve stamina, and improve speed. Exercises repeated in the varying motions of any given sport help the body learn to do these motions. It also learns to combine the various motions into one smooth, overall act, thereby increasing coordination.

As far as stamina goes, repeating the act in ever-increasing frequency or over an ever-increasing span of time improves the ability of the body to carry on beyond its expected limits. This includes the ability to control breathing and facilitate exchange of oxygen in the body. The performance can now be carried out under more difficult conditions, and for a longer period of time.

Finally, repetitive action and increasing the tone of muscles through conditioning causes an increase in the speed at which various activities can be carried out. This includes not only running but hand speed and general body speed in the coordinated movements of any given sport.

Mental conditioning

Mental conditioning is equally important. You're taking an individual and teaching him to become part of a unit. Even in the sports that are not considered to be team sports, you are teaching him discipline, especially in today's permissive society.

It might be a young athlete's first contact with discipline. Previously he might have done pretty much as he pleased. Now he has to subordinate his own desires to the good of the group. He has to learn to suffer today to attain rewards tomorrow, and somewhere he learns that this is what life really is all about.

It's never too early to begin to teach children about sports and, in doing so at a young age, you are conditioning them. It becomes a question of degree and approach.

I don't approve of a highly competitive situation where young people have a tendency to burn themselves out physically and mentally. I think it's good if you get a bunch of young people and let them play, and teach them how to play properly without organized leagues. Children having fun playing don't get tired of the idea as much as children who are under pressure to win.

There is an interesting league in Philadelphia where all the children of the same age are put in a pool and re-selected every week so the teams are constantly changing. Even the coaching staffs move from one team to another. Everyone plays, everyone has fun, and apparently the level of skills is about the same as in organized Little Leagues. The difference is that the injury rate drops off significantly in this type of competition.

Actually, the children have never been the problem, but rather the adults and their competitive desires. In my hometown we have a league in which everyone *has to play at least three innings,* and has to come to bat at least once. It's still a competitive situation of winning and losing, but it's a lot different from nine players going out there and fighting for the reputation of the dear old coach.

This is a lot different from an athlete dedicating himself to deliver 100 percent of his ability, as we see when we go further into the various aspects of mental conditioning.

17
Diet: The care and feeding of the engine

Experience by a great many persons in the field of conditioning has developed a set of guidelines and rules. Maximum benefit will come from following these closely.

Let's start with the two basics—sleep and food.

Sleep

Sleep is the master body-builder. If you're tired, there's no question—you can't perform. A young person has to have sleep and rest in order to grow and function properly. If you're playing hard you have to renew your body strength, and sleep is the only way. There are no set hours; you'll know when you've had too little.

Food

Food is a matter of balanced diets vs. food fads and supplements. Some of the supplements may become necessary in special instances, but there is no substitute for eating well.

Fads are all the looney diets for slimming down. Basically, the teenage diet is probably the worst in the world, counting heavily on such items as french fries, pizza, and soft drinks. It won't do. You have to go with a balanced diet. You need grain cereals, vegetables, fruits, and eggs and other proteins.

The high school athlete is notoriously a poor eater because he skips breakfast. Or, maybe he has a roll and coffee and calls it breakfast. It is very important that the body be revitalized after a night's rest.

Then the average high school athlete lives the rest of the day on sandwiches and junk food. He often eats only one balanced meal a day, that being dinner at home. If you eat a basically well-balanced diet, you don't need vitamins but, since most don't, probably vitamins are not a bad thing.

Gaining weight

We come to individual weight. There are certain boys who simply can't fill out and gain, no matter what and how much they eat. There are high protein food supplements put out by reputable health food companies that are mixed with milk and taken as a supplement to the normal diet, *not instead of.* These can add 1,500 calories a day and can be helpful in putting on some poundage over a couple of months. Caution: Don't use a food supplement instead of a meal.

We live in a weight-oriented society where almost everyone you speak to is trying to *lose* weight. It is unusual when we find someone trying to gain. An athlete might be trying to pick up weight in order to play the sport he's picked. He might not be big enough.

Weight again depends on an increase of caloric intake with high calorie foods like starches, sugars, and some fats. If you take in more than you burn up during the day you'll gain; if you take in less you'll lose. Even if the extra calories come from bread, cake, ice cream, jelly, butter, honey on pancakes, etc., you will gain weight. However, to build muscle tissue you need protein, and that comes from meat, eggs, cheese, and milk. You also have to balance your diet with vegetables and fruit for vitamin intake.

If an athlete can't gain on the above type of regimen, a diet should be tailored for him by his doctor.

Losing weight

For *losing* weight, we simply turn the program around. Reduce the intake below the expenditure level. Concentrate on protein because the body can't burn protein.

Milk is nature's most nearly perfect food. It has the protein and calcium you need for building body tissue. Diets have to include a lot of protein to make muscle. All athletes should be milk drinkers. If there is an overweight problem or a history of high cholesterol in the family, switch to skimmed milk.

And don't forget good old orange juice, the great refresher. Nothing cuts the fatigue and the dust in your throat and takes care of the dry mouth like orange juice. It is also a great replenisher of some of the vital body substances lost in large amounts during periods of heavy sweating.

18
The legs, your most important asset in sports

The legs

If winning is 40 percent conditioning, then running enjoys a similar percentage in relation to conditioning. You can skip a number of important things and still get by if you run, run, run. Running builds your legs, and there is no sport that doesn't depend basically on your legs. Running also builds up your wind. "Wind"—that's what you have, or haven't, in the fourth period of a game.

In running, as in most physical activity, form is important. Keep relaxed. Don't fight yourself. Tension pits the extensor muscles against the flexors with tremendous loss of efficiency. Thus, all the muscles are working against one another. When you're loose, only the muscles that are going where you want to go are put into play. Don't clench your fists. It interferes with arm action. Keep your elbows in and synchronize your arm action with your legs. Don't be bull-doggish about it. Just relax.

For speed training, start with short sprints of 10 or 20 yards, then work up to 40. Forty yards is the basic sprint in football. A player's speed in that sport is rated over that distance.

For endurance, drive, and agility, try running up and down stadium steps. Run up short, steep hills. This develops maximum leg drive over short distances. This exercise is good for the fullback who needs maximum explosive effort over short distances. Running on the beach, in soft sand or in the shallow water, gives you the resistance that strengthens the foot and arch. It's better than ankle-weight type of resistance.

Practice acceleration sprints. This starts with a sprint at maximum speed for 20 yards, alternating with a 20-yard walk, back to sprinting, etc., all for a total of 100 yards. This builds endurance.

In practice, start thinking in terms of exploding, nonelevation, and extension. This means coming off the blocks (or other start) concentrating to the maximum on the first step and keeping low. You extend your body out forward in that crouch, leaning forward. For football linemen this will put the athlete right into the middle of the opposing linemen, which is where he is supposed to be. For the runner it means he has cut down his wind resistance and he's got the first few steps out of the way.

Running improves agility. Many boys have poor coordination initially. A famous athlete once observed, "In high school I couldn't get from the dressing room to the bench without getting hurt." Training and conditioning changed him over.

To help develop agility, practice running backwards, something football and basketball players must learn. This calls for a quick start, and stop, using 10- and 20-yard sprints, forward *and* backward.

One of the greatest agility developers is the so-called six-seconds drill, originally designed for football. It was based on the theory that no play in football lasts more than six seconds, unless it goes 90 yards for a touchdown. Normally there is a 30-second rest between plays.

We have a group following the leader in a maximum amount of rolls, turns, drops, bounces—all crammed into six seconds. Thereafter, the playing time in a real game doesn't seem as long.

Spinning and turning is an important part of running training. You take quarter-turns at a quick pace, beginning by running forward, then turning and running sideways, always in a straight line. Do this upright and on all fours. The fours is very difficult but rewarding.

There is a drill for recovery from being off balance. You run ten yards, drop one hand to the ground, run a circle around that hand; then reverse—get up and run another ten yards, drop the other hand down and run around *that* one.

For lateral agility we have the carioca, a Pan-American dance popular 40 years ago (you can see it in old movies with Fred Astaire and Ginger Rogers on TV). This is the end stage of "spinning and turning." You turn and reverse *every other* step. Very difficult but absolutely essential for the defensive football player.

In the "crossover" we are running backward, crossing our feet to change direction. Any good defensive back in football or soccer has to be able to do this with tremendous speed and drive. A basketball player on defense is called upon to do this. In baseball you see an outfielder backpedal a little, then suddenly turn and go to the wall. You have to be able to maneuver like this without getting your feet tangled up. It's very easy to collapse in an embarrassed heap if you don't know your business here.

In the agility department there's nothing like jumping rope, one of the world's greatest drills for this particular talent. Do it five minutes and increase eventually to 15 minutes. Go in both directions, forward and backward.

Agility goes beyond balance on your feet. It means falling properly too. The difference in knowing how to fall and how not to fall could mean the difference between a year in action and a year on the bench. Broken wrists, dislocated elbows, dislocated shoulders, shoulder separations are all caused by falling on the outstretched arm.

The secret of a "successful" fall is relaxation but still maintaining control of the body. Once you're falling, you can't "fight it." You have to practice the forward and backward roll, head tucked so that you don't land on the top of your head. You have to practice coming down on your shoulder with your elbows tucked in. Your natural instinct is to put out your hand to break your fall. Don't do it. Pull that hand and elbow back in. Come down and roll.

19
The other fellow is even more tired

For endurance an athlete should run, run, run, and when very tired, then he should run some more. If you run out of room to run, run in place. Nothing can take the place of running for improving an athlete's condition.

Swimming, too, is an excellent overall conditioner. At one time it was frowned upon by coaches in contact sports because it was felt swimming had a bad effect on muscle tone. We know now that body fluids should be replaced after heavy exercise, and in salt water the body will absorb minerals and water through the skin.

Proper warm-ups are necessary to prevent injury. A gradual increase in body temperature loosens muscle fibers. By increasing the blood supply and by contraction (which is work), you give off heat. This allows the muscle to stretch more easily. Gradual stretching and loosening combine to avoid tears and pulls. The increased blood supply carries more oxygen and nutrition to the muscle and permits it to perform more efficiently.

Salt intake is extremely important and must be considered. A number of athletic deaths, reported annually as "heat deaths," are basically deaths due to loss of salt and water.

Large amounts of salt and water are lost through exercise and sweating. Their loss leads to loss of strength and lower performance. In this situation the muscle tissue itself suffers cramps. Legs knot up. Intestinal cramps may result.

In heat stroke it becomes impossible to function at all. The victim becomes out of breath. He sweats, he becomes very hot and, finally, lapses into unconsciousness or even death.

In warm weather, it is necessary to build up the salt and water reserve in the body prior to

Standard endurance program (excellent for pre-season conditioning)

Exercise	Increases by week (four-week program)		
One 440 yard lap (walk, trot, stride)	+2		
Four 50-yard dashes	+6	8	10
Two 100-yard strides, half speed	+3	4	5
One 440-yard trot	+2	3	4
Ten pushups	+15	20	25
Six chinups	+8	10	12
Ten sit-ups	+15	20	25
Ten horizontal runs, 10 yards (on all fours)	+15	15	20
Five minutes rope skipping	+10	10	20

exercise. Even more important is maintaining the level of potassium in the body. It is not a good practice to take large amounts of salt tablets prior to exercise or during exercise. It has been found that the high concentrations of salt cause more trouble to the body than the possible benefits they bring. The answer to the problem is in the use of commercial preparations—Gatorade, Sportade, and the many other preparations that are available to give the body a measured blend of water and minerals; these are readily absorbed and rapidly replace the body's loss.

Although these preparations are more expensive than salt tablets and water, they are not prohibitive and should be considered as necessary as the mandatory equipment in any sport in order to make participation safe. The old theory that water taken during practice or during a game will make you ill has gone by the boards. It is necessary to make frequent stops for water or commercial drinks during practice, even as often as every ten or fifteen minutes if the weather is hot and the practice is heavy.

Unfortunately, there are still coaches who insist that their players not take water during practice. This can be an extremely serious mistake, perhaps fatal to an athlete if the weather is sufficiently hot.

20
Giving up today's pleasure for tomorrow's reward

Young athletes the world over, and for a lot longer than the authors have been around, have been faced with the decision posed by the heading of this chapter. Do you want it today and forget about tomorrow, or can you look ahead for rewards that are infinitely greater than the ones you seem to have in your hand? Winning in sports demands total dedication—learning to deliver 100 percent of your ability. There's no other way, despite the star with unorthodox ways who blazes across the sport's horizon for a while, then flames out almost as dramatically as he came.

The mental aspect of conditioning is every bit as important as the physical. Dedication, concentration, maturity, knowledge, understanding—all these qualities are as important as the ability to move with the crack of the bat, read defenses, block a puck, lay one up.

In concentration, a young athlete must realize that all star performers have one trait in common, an ability to blot out everything that doesn't matter or that doesn't have any effect on what's going on. Noise in the stands rolls off him, other players' taunts fall upon ears buttoned down as far as the opposition is concerned.

Young persons have comparatively short concentration spans and must work constantly on increasing them. You can't succeed when you perform 90 percent and miss out on the other 10 percent due to loss of concentration.

Young athletes must develop the ability to make mature judgments from the circumstances they face at the moment. They must be aware of what's going on around them and adjust to come up with their best performance. Concentration, dedication, and maturity will bring confidence, and a confident athlete is a better athlete.

Stars are great, but early a young athlete has to develop the ability to sacrifice for the good of the team, to pass off to someone else rather than take a chance on scoring himself from a more difficult spot. It's teamwork vs. individuality—and teamwork wins games.

Young athletes have to learn to control their emotions during stress and pressure. You can't win the game sitting on the bench after you've been thrown out for fighting. One of the hardest things to teach a young athlete is to walk away from a fight. If you're a good player, the other team may be trying to get you out of the game this way. Don't strike back because the referee just might have missed the earlier swipe that caused you to retaliate.

A young athlete must know the rules and shouldn't depend on absorbing them naturally. It's all written down in books—what you can and can't do. Take a look once in a while. If game officials study the rule book nightly, you certainly can afford the time to look up something that's bothering you, and even something that isn't.

You have to learn to anticipate ("What do I do if the ball is hit to me now?"). Learn what to expect of the opposition. Study the opposition. Is the second baseman shading too far over. Does the forward blink before he passes off? Learn never to underestimate the opposition, no matter what the previous record has been. Everything is ancient history once the new game begins.

Above all, develop understanding. Know *why* you're doing something at a particular time. It's great to have a strong belief in your coach and belief in your team captain and in what they say, but sometimes they may not be right. No one *is* right 100 percent of the time.

Maybe you can do the same thing they're asking in another way and do it a little better. You're not being advised to question every little thing that comes up. But understand why you're doing what you're doing. And, if you think there's a better way, try to suggest it without hurting anyone's feelings. Feelings will be hurt a lot more if a close game is lost.

It is of considerable importance that young athletes be aware of the tremendous importance of attitude. In other words, a player should be encouraged to go out and do his very best and not be handcuffed by the fear of possibly making a mistake. Many players, with the choice of trying something difficult, would rather not do anything because of the possible consequences of a mistake.

You see this in the basketball player who has an open shot and doesn't take it because he is afraid of missing in a crucial situation. It should be impressed on young athletes that they go out and do the best they can and not worry about mistakes.

21
Ninety-pound weaklings are rarely all-Americans

Weight lifting

Weight lifting changed my life, and although it might not have such a dramatic impact on yours, it could make your career as an athlete a different and better one. Weight lifting enabled me to play high school football after being ignored in my first year because I was too light and small. From there I went on to a career as a major league defensive back with the New York Giants.

Through a weight lifting program I put on 40 pounds in one year in high school. I went from 135 pounds as a freshman to 175 as a sophomore, and any doubts the coach had in my first year vanished when he saw me come back after a summer of weights. Weight lifting also gave me the stamina to take the knocks and blows of college and pro football. I can't recommend it enthusiastically enough for young persons starting on athletic careers.

Weight lifting has been practiced for a long time. I suppose Hercules would fall into the category of a weight lifter, along with that other mythological character, Atlas. As a young fellow I used to see the Charles Atlas (no relation) ads, with the fingers grasped, the forearm and shoulder muscles bulging. This dynamic tension was the forerunner of isometrics, which is the use of one muscle group against another group of muscles to stimulate increased strength in both.

The idea of muscles on athletes goes back to the first Olympic games, the original ones. A stronger athlete has always been a better one, and muscles denote strength.

Today, track men have to build their bodies if they plan to play football or other contact games. Muscle bulk is needed to protect the bony structures of the body from the blows that inevitably come in contact sports.

Weight training is better than straight calisthenics for building body bulk and strength. Calisthenics loosen and warm up the body and tend to help the body keep its tone, but a tremendous amount of calisthenics is needed to build body tissue. Weight training gives you bulk along with strength of muscle.

Effort applied repeatedly to a muscle gives increasing bulk, vitality, elasticity, and strength. Together, their combined effect is also increased stamina. Sometimes the overall change—body size alone—is amazing.

Weight training is divided into two classes, muscle building and muscle toning. Toning follows building, naturally. You have to have something to tone.

Muscle building

Building means using heavy weight with few repetitions. Simply, it means lifting 100 pounds three times, rather than three pounds 100 times. The heavy lift taxes the muscle beyond what it can do easily and is the direct cause of the increase in the number of muscle fiber cells, which brings a consequent increase in strength. In muscle building you are constantly calling upon the muscle groups always to do slightly more than they are capable of doing easily.

Here, we run into a longstanding problem: What is *too much?* Too much weight can cause injury through the tearing of muscle groups that are forced beyond the limit of their capacity. Weight training should be under the direction of someone who has had long experience in knowing limits.

If such direction isn't available, increases in weight should be done by small amounts so that the body is always being pushed slightly, and is *never* overloaded with large amounts of excess efforts. The latter cannot only cause injury but can dampen a young person's enthusiasm in a hurry.

Muscle toning

Toning's function is similar to calisthenics. Once you have the muscle you have to keep it toned to keep its performance level at its peak and to prevent muscle-tissue breakdown simply from disuse. Here, small weights used many times is the program—the three pounds lifted 100 times.

This gives us the two concepts necessary for a successful weight lifting program, the heavy stuff and the light stuff, few times, many times.

A vital partner to a weight lifting program is a heavy diet of running. The weight lifting is adding bulk and weight to your body, which is immediately faced with the problem of moving this increased weight from one place to the other, sometimes at top speed. The respiratory system also has to face the same challenge. The leg muscles you had only a few months ago might balk and finally quit under the new load unless they've been brought along on a program to build them, too.

A running program should include a warm-up period to increase the blood supply and relax and heat the muscles at the beginning of each workout. You must always remember the increased amount of muscle calls for a markedly increased circulatory supply in the body. This warm-up should include jogging and repeated sprints.

Your legs are your prime possession in any athletic effort. If weight training brings increased bulk but causes a loss of speed, you've gained nothing, maybe even taken a backward step. The program must balance. As a 160-pounder you have to go from first to second base, or go in to make the layup just as fast and as agilely as you did as a 130-pounder.

Additionally, the legs must be built up for the following five reasons:

1. There must be ability for quick starting and stopping (the quick start and stop depend on the "drive train" of the leg, that group of muscles from the Achilles tendon through the calf, the thigh and into the gluteal area).

2. There must be ability to change direction rapidly (change of direction depends on the lower leg, the arch of the foot and its ability to grip the ground, and the calf area in the new push-off).

3. There must be ability to spin and turn (spinning and turning depend on the waist

and lower back control, as well as the leg muscles).

4. There must be overall coordination in running.

5. There must be ability to recover from being off balance or stumbling (coordination and balance recovery depend on a coordinated effort and strength in all the muscles of the leg).

There are other general rules to be observed in weight work before we go into more specific areas like the exercises themselves. In breathing, the Golden Rule is to inhale during the maximum exertion in the exercise and exhale during the return to the starting position. You should always be deliberate, *never* spasmodic, and the lift should be done in a steady rhythmic pace.

Never hurry, rest sufficiently between each exercise, and make sure you feel you have recovered. Don't do weight lifting daily. You'll find you'll get more out of a program of three times a week than if you lift daily.

There are two types of weight-training equipment. One is the Olympic bar, which is a steel bar or axle on which weight plates can be added or taken off on either end. The whole apparatus is lifted.

The second is the Universal station machine, which has a series of "stations" at which all possible exercises can be done. Each "station" offers a particular type of equipment with varying weights. Weights are stacked and can be quickly switched. This is a superior concept in mass training. It allows up to twelve persons to use the equipment.

And now a quick look into the grocery department before moving into actual exercises. Weight lifting calls for an increase in food intake in order that nourishment will be available to produce the new muscle fibers. The diet should be very high in protein, the main substance for forming body muscle tissue. There should also be a high intake of starches and sugars, needed to supply the energy to carry out the exercise program being attempted.

Weight lifting exercises

As in the earlier portion of this book, we'll move from the foot upward, making key stops at the various sections of the body. The weights suggested are averages and should be adjusted downward if you can't handle them.

Toe raises

Use a 2 x 4 board on the floor; stand with your toes on the board and your heels on the floor. Start with 100 pounds resting on your shoulders behind your neck. The bar should be wrapped with a towel, taped on, so that you won't risk bruising your neck or back. As a matter of fact, *all* lifting exercises should have a wrapped bar. It can't hurt.

Try to increase the weight by ten pounds every two or three weeks. The repetition here is eight to twelve times, increasing as you feel the need. This exercise is used to develop the calf, put the spring into your legs, and help your body balance.

You raise your heels off the ground onto the balls of your feet, thus stretching the Achilles tendon, the ankles, and the arches. Lift in a slow rhythm to get the most out of it. This exercise can be done in three ways—your feet straight, pigeon-toed, or duck feet (45-degree angle). Straight develops the back of the calf, pigeon-toed the outside of the calf, and duck feet the inside of the calf.

Three-quarters knee bend

As in all conditioning there is no place for a full squat in weight lifting. It damages the knee and loosens the cartilage and ligaments. And don't try any duck walks.

The three-quarters knee bend lift develops leg power and strength and also helps back strength. It'll increase lung capacity and will help put weight on your thighs.

It's done with the weight on the back of the neck. You take the bar from the stand, then place it on the back of your neck. Your feet should be 12 to 14 inches apart, heels flat on the ground, toes slightly out. Your shoulders are back, head and chin up. Inhale as you go down, exhale as you go up.

Rowing

Your feet are about 2½ inches apart for this one, knees straight but not stiff. The palms should be facing toward the legs. Grab the bar about the width of the shoulders.

We're talking about a lift of from 80 to 100 pounds. Pull the weight up to your chest; inhale as you go up, exhale as you go down. It develops your upper back muscles, gives your arms pulling power and shoulders a definite snap. It also strengthens your wrists and fingers. This is a good exercise for baseball players. You are developing chest, arms, and upper back—good development for batting muscles in baseball.

Stiff leg dead lift

Start with 100 pounds; increase weight every two weeks. The bar is on the floor. Place your feet under the bar, knees straight but not stiff, arms straight but not stiff, and grasp the bar in the middle. Straighten the back to an upright position, holding the weights.

At the top of the exercise, when the weight is all the way up to your waist, throw the chest out. Breathe, inhale as you come up, exhale as you go down. Lowering the weight, keep the same control of the position of the body as when raising the weights.

This strengthens your lower back, your shoulders, your arms, and your wrists because of the weight you're pulling up. It also stretches the hamstring muscle of your posterior thigh. These are muscles that hardly ever get stretched. It's important for these muscles to get some development because when we get into starting and stopping in competition, these are the muscles that are subject to pulls.

Bench press

The aim here is to develop the upper body and shoulders. You lie on the bench with your feet straddling the bench, and the weight resting on your chest. Or, you take it off a platform. The weight here varies. You can start with half your body weight or go to 80 to 100 pounds. The repetitions are 8 to 12.

Lie flat on your back, heels on the ground; grasp the bar on the outside edge. Keep your elbows out wide, along the line of the bar. *Don't* grab the bar too close to your chest.

Raise the weights up and inhale, extending the elbows to the maximum. Exhale coming down. What you are doing here is developing the upper body and chest, mainly the chest. Deep breathing is the important thing here.

Dead lift

Place the feet under the bar and about 12 inches apart. Both are pointed slightly outward. Bend from a ½ or ¾ squat. Heels are down. Bend the knees so you can reach the bar. Now raise it with arms straight to standing position. The head should be up, and inhale as you go up. Lower the bar to the ground, bending the knees only. Do not bend backward. Be in the same body position as when you started. Exhale going down.

This is the best all-around weight exercise and the best power exercise for the neck, arms, and the lower back. We are talking about a weight of 150 pounds, and a variation could be ¾ of your body weight. Add 10 pounds every two weeks. This is good for the lower back. It stretches the lower muscles and helps when you get into running.

Behind-the-neck press

This lift is good right after you do your toe raises. The weight is on the back of your neck. Extend your arms over your head, then bring the weight back down onto the shoulders and back of the neck. We're talking about 110 pounds and repetitions of 8 to 10. This develops the muscle between your neck and shoulder and it is also beneficial for the deltoid. The behind-the-neck press is good exercise for football and hockey players.

Military press

This is done upright. You take the weight from the floor, bringing it up to the chest with the palms facing outward. Inhale as you raise the weight over your head; exhale as you bring it back down to the chest. This is a 1-2 operation. It develops your arms and chest. Actually, it is a stand-up bench press, and it's good for baseball, tennis, and wrestling.

Shoulder shrug

The weight should be held groin high for this one. You're just holding the weight in your hands, not wide, not too short, but sort of in line with your shoulders. Now you just shrug your shoulders, inhaling as you do so. This develops the muscle between your neck and shoulder and your trapezius, which is your "side" muscle. This could be called the "I don't know why I'm doing this" training exercise—the shrugger. It's a good developer and provides for rapid muscle development.

Jumping jacks

Bring as much weight as you're comfortable with up to the back of the neck. You now jump out and extend your legs outward, then jump again and bring your legs together. It's good for basketball players. Do this 8 to 10 times. Don't forget the towel wrapping on the bar.

Yoga breathing

This is something I learned as a young person in Connecticut—a long way from the Orient where the exercise originates. It's the perfect relaxer, good for the chest and the stomach, and ties in with weight lifting, before and after. You stand erect comfortably. Exhale after taking one breath and concentrate on blowing all the air out of your lungs until you feel you can't blow out any more. Now you should feel as though your stomach is somewhere around your backbone.

Now, slo-o-o-ow-lyyy, inhale all the air you can, keeping your head up, expanding your chest. When you feel you simply can't inhale any more, exhale rapidly. Then you relax.

Do this 2 or 3 times before and after your regular weight exercise. This is also beneficial to people who aren't weight lifting, but who need a relaxer.

Tired legs and feet

When the blood supply gets to your lower extremities, it tends to stick around there a while. Occasionally it's good to move the blood so some fresh stuff can get in. For this, a head stand of five minutes and a lot of deep breathing is recommended.

Put a pillow under your head, put your hands on the floor, and raise your legs up to the wall. Do this right next to the wall for obvious reasons. The blood will come out of your lower extremities into your chest and a lot of it is going into your head too, which is good. A less drastic position is the one where you are reclining and you elevate your feet 45 degrees. This gets the old stuff out and the new stuff in.

Results

The preceding exercises, which basically comprise my own weight lifting routine, should help some young athlete become better than he normally would have become. I know it worked that way for me.

Keep a goal in mind. Measure yourself for height, weight, and the dimensions of the parts of your body you want to develop. Remember you're striving to be better than average.

Instant success will not come. But, in a week or two you'll start noticing change. And, after 30 days you'll see a pleasing increase. Above all, your mental attitude has to be a positive one. You *know* you'll benefit from lifting weights.

New developments

A word now on the advances in weight work—equipment which was not available to athletes of a generation ago. These are the weight machines, which are isokinetic, as compared to the task of lifting different weights, which is in the isotonic category. The best known of these are the Nautilus, the Mini-Gym, and the Orthotron.

These machines are sophisticated equipment with eccentric cams or hydraulic systems that make possible the changing of the load on the muscle as it lifts, keeping it fully loaded as it moves through the entire range of motion. The standard lifting equipment cannot do this. Here, you are limited by the amount of weight that can be lifted in the weakest area in the range of motion. The machines provide for a more efficient expenditure of energy because the muscle is working at 100 percent of capacity throughout the entire exercise.

Additionally, the Orthotron has one other advantage over the others. It can be set to move at any given speed or "explosion," meaning the maximum effort at high speed for the initial push-off, such as a sprinter starting in track, or any other sport where the first two steps are important.

These machines, all of them, are extremely expensive and can't be used at home. Since they are designed to accommodate one small area of the body, there may be a need for as many as twenty of them. Thus, we have weight centers springing up all over the country where athletes may work on these machines at a comparatively inexpensive rate. They are valuable for all athletes, but especially for the budding ones. If you have a machine available, it is not a bad idea to work and weight train under the guidance of an instructor.

22
One after meals and one at bedtime

A slightly less-than-great TV announcer, defending his full-time job of describing sporting events for a very good living, declared, "Sports are a microcosm of our society," and then turned around to butter up some athlete who banked a half-million the previous year. That may be a microcosm, but it isn't reflecting the situation around the average high school or middle-class suburb. He'd have been a lot more honest had he declared that sports has much the same problems that society has—and up there on the list are drugs and a sometimes unwise dependence on medication, some of it self-prescribed.

One good way to look at the picture is to think that whenever you put a drug or some medication into your body it will have some effect, favorable you hope. And for that effect or action there will ultimately be a reaction. And what we are hoping here is that the action will outweigh the reaction.

Let's have a look, beginning with the mildest and working up to the strongest of narcotics and stimulants.

Vitamins

We start with the simplest of medications we can put into an athlete's body. That would be vitamins, and maybe the second or third generation of athletes are now using these.

There is no real evidence that an athlete needs higher doses of vitamins than does the average person. If he eats a well-balanced diet, there really isn't any need for vitamin supplements for an athlete. If he is dieting to lose weight, to get into condition, or to keep his weight down (such as in making a weight class in wrestling), then it becomes important for an athlete to be on a vitamin supplement. This is because with the above restrictions he may not be getting adequate vitamins in his everyday diet.

If an athlete's resistance is down it is felt that certain of the vitamins will help him maintain an adequate state of health. It's been my feeling that a good, high-potency multiple vitamin is the best answer to the problem and that the combination of specific vitamins taken by many athletes really is of no value. Combinations used in high-potency products are more than adequate. In addition, the fad in vitamins swings through the years. There really has been no scientific evidence that vitamins have made a good athlete any better than he normally would have been.

Vitamin E, now in high favor, is a typical example. There's no evidence that E does anything in the body or that there is an established need for it. Outside of increasing fertility in rats, no specific action has been found for E. Yet, it is described as a panacea for a million illnesses to which athletes are prone.

Go one step further and view the use of B_{12} shots for energy. Another bit of totally wasted effort for the athlete. The common impression is it gives you energy, but this stems from its use in pernicious anemia where people striken complain of extreme tiredness. They feel more energetic after a B_{12} shot. In the absence of anemia, B_{12} has absolutely no effect on energy level.

Steroids

In an entirely different class are the steroids, the cortisones and cortisone shots. These are among the most potent of medications and, with antibiotics, have to rank with twentieth-century miracles. Their curative powers in inflammations, tendinitis, bursitis, and arthritis is truly amazing. Severely disabled areas can be relieved in a matter of 48 hours and an athlete can be returned to activity.

However, if administered incorrectly, steroids can have severe side effects. Taken orally, cortisone can have an effect on the blood sugar, blood pressure, water metabolism, and the entire glandular structure. So, it is imperative that an athlete *not* treat himself with cortisone given him by someone else. He should take it only as prescribed and only for the period of time prescribed. There are many systemic diseases in which the use of cortisone could be fatal.

Cortisone by injection poses a slightly different problem. This is not the panacea of all ailments and should not be used indiscriminately by doctors who are unaware of possible complications in athletes. Cortisone injections should be reserved for bursitis, tendinitis, and joint cavities where inflammation has set up and where oral drugs aren't potent enough. Depot types of cortisone cut down on side effects because they are not well absorbed, so these are somewhat safer to use.

Under proper medical supervision, however, cortisone is safe. It is probably the single most important drug we have in the treatment of athletic injuries. No reason exists to resist the use of these drugs by a physician. However, if unsupervised, there is hardly anything more dangerous.

Another drug with much of the same effect is Butazolidin, which is outstanding in the treatment of inflammations such as tendinitis, myositis, and bursitis. It can be used in cases where cortisone can't be used.

Butazolidin must never be taken unless under strict medical supervision. Rare but serious complications can result from such indiscriminate use as finishing off the last few pills remaining from a teammate's prescription.

Supervision usually means frequent blood checks because of the possibility, however remote, of aplastic anemia.

Anabolic steroids, or weight-gaining pills, are now completely in disfavor. They were formerly used widely because of their ability to pack on tremendous muscle mass and bulk via the medication and an accompanying diet. Weight gains of 30 or 40 pounds of solid muscle, not fat, were not unknown, and weight lifters were some of the most enthusiastic users.

Then it became clear that these weight-gaining pills were not without side effects. At the top of the list were items like loss of sex drive, voice change, hair pattern change on the body, and a general reshuffling of the secondary sex characteristics. Among women these drugs had a definite masculinizing effect. It was discovered that football players taking this medication had a tendency to bone problems via a softening of the long bones. The drugs have been mentioned in expensive damage suits by pro football players claiming that these pills led to a shortening of their careers.

The medical profession has universally condemned the use of these drugs. Today, the only athletes taking them are some weight lifters and shot putters, and they are doing it on their own via black-market sources.

Aspirin

Right here, a word to parents might be appropriate concerning medication. Know what your child is taking, and ask—even to the point of making a nuisance of yourself. And, when a child goes to see a physician because of an athletic injury or condition, a parent should go along. Only then will it be definite that the medication taken came from the proper source.

Aspirin might be the one exception. It is the most widely used of all pain and discomfort factor eliminators. It has great affinity for joint problems. Why, we don't know. And, it is probably the most effective agent in arthritis and joint pain. It's been around a long time, going back to the late nineteenth century, and its mystery is as deep as when it was first introduced.

There are side effects from *large* doses of aspirin, or heavy frequency of use. Gastric upset can develop, along with heartburn and even bleeding from irritation of the stomach lining. Larger doses can cause ringing of the ears and dizziness, and there is the danger of developing a tendency to bleed, also from heavy dosages. But "a couple of aspirin" never killed anyone. Just make sure that it's aspirin your child is taking.

Amphetamines—uppers

There is a group of drugs known as uppers, speed, greenies, pep pills. Their use, which has spread rapidly among athletes, cause them to warrant a good long look and discussion. Basically, these are Benzedrine-based derivatives which increase a feeling of well-being and provide a feeling of strength in the body. People suddenly feel they can accomplish physical feats from which they've backed off previously.

This action apparently comes through an increase in the heart rate, which steps up the blood rate in the body and, in that sense, gets more oxygen into the vital muscle areas. The drug causes an increased activity in the nervous system.

Uppers represent more problems than they are worth. Long studies of athletes under the influence of these drugs indicate that while they *feel* they are stronger and more proficient, there is *no* evidence of increased productivity or ability. If anything, there is a marked *decrease* in the performance under the influence, due to the interferences in timing and reaction with the central nervous system stimulation.

An example is recalled of the quarterback who was extremely accurate in practice but was ten yards too long with his passes in the game. He took a "pep" pill prior to the game because it made him "feel stronger" but it actually spoiled his timing to the extent that he was constantly overthrowing.

In addition, the increase of metabolism in the body because of pep pills may effectively mask severe fatigue in the late stages of the game when the athlete should be getting warning signals from his body that he'd better think about slowing down a bit. He keeps going on a full head of steam and this leaves him open to disabling fatigue after his performance. In larger doses it leads to confusion and lack of good judgment as well as interfering with reflexes and instinct. If taken with any degree of regularity, the drug becomes something the body depends on in order to perform. Increased doses become necessary to maintain that original feeling of superiority.

All drugs in this classification, additionally, are appetite depressants, so the nutrition of the body is ignored. Therefore, on one end we have over-stimulation and, on the other end, under-nourishment.

When the drugs are stopped, there is invariably a depression and lack of productivity in the athlete. Flat out, these drugs have *no place under any circumstances* in the athletic world, and banning them has been one of the wisest steps taken in sports medicine.

Depressants—downers

On the other end of the stick from the uppers are the *downers*—depressants such as barbiturates, sleeping pills, and tranquilizers. These take an athlete, or anyone else, "out of it"—no worries and no pressures, just a numb unawareness. They work on the central nervous system, decreasing its activity.

Downers have no function for an athlete. Naturally, they will cause a definite reduction in his reaction to the point where he could sustain severe injury by not responding rapidly enough to any given situation. His nervous system isn't functioning properly, and he will drop markedly in performance.

In addition, addiction becomes a severe problem. It is easy to become dependent, and with that dependency comes a need for more medication as the body becomes more tolerant of it. So, there is that never-ending circle again. Withdrawal from barbiturates and tranquilizers is much more difficult than withdrawal from other narcotics, and there is the possibility of death during this process even though heroin withdrawals, for example, have been more highly publicized. It is recommended urgently that these drugs be avoided at all costs.

Alcohol

The depressant with the highest visibility is alcohol. Alcohol affects the central nervous system. This is born out by a simple experiment; drink enough and you become so depressed that you become unconscious, the ultimate depressed condition.

The feeling of well-being from alcohol comes from its ability to depress the centers of the brain first. The highest centers are the ones most easily depressed. This allows freedom for the animal-like instincts that we normally keep in check. There is a marked change of personality among some persons under the influence of alcohol.

Among hockey players there is a strong feeling that post-game beer is the best possible fluid replacement following the heavy sweating during a contest. And when used in a social situation, most people feel that alcohol in moderation is not harmful to mature (physically and mentally) individuals.

During working hours, however, alcohol interferes with timing, reflexes, and sound judgment. Heavy use cuts down on the appetite, and the lack of adequate food intake can lead to serious conditions such as cirrhosis of the liver. Impairment of judgment, on the field and off, can cause injury.

It is not suggested here that every top athlete is a teetotaler. Some of the greatest in the world have been known to take a drink, but the question is whether they might not have been greater without it.

Cocaine, heroin

Cocaine and heroin are substances which hold no place in the field of athletics. They destroy the nervous system ultimately, and the impairment of performance is instant.

There is no possible way anyone can perform under the influence of such a narcotic. Even after the direct effects have subsided, it is impossible to perform because of the withdrawal symptoms. In this case, the body is either depressed or agitated, and an athlete can hardly expect to perform at his best when in either of these states.

Among the most destructive consequences of narcotics are: the tendency of the user to ignore eating, the possibility of an overdose, an infection from impure narcotics, or a disabling case of hepatitis through infection via unclean syringes. These are hardly routes worth traveling.

It can't be emphasized strongly enough how the cards are stacked against anyone who even experiments. This is because of the rapid addiction to heroin and the extremely low recovery rate. There are very few narcotic addicts who don't go back to using the drug when the going gets rough and the stress seems unbearable. We don't seem to be able to really cure drug addiction too well. There are very few *old* addicts. Usually they don't live that long.

Marijuana

We come now to marijuana, a drug with which the average high school athlete is more familiar than is his parent. There are as yet no hard and true facts on marijuana and its effects on the body over a long period. Some feel there is a genetic deficiency that develops through the use of "pot" which leads to a higher incidence of abnormal babies. Whether this can be transmitted from a man who has been a marijuana smoker is not yet known.

Marijuana *does* impair performance while a person is under its influence just as any other depressant, like alcohol, causes impairment. Again, any permanent effect has not been proven. But, look at all the years tobacco was smoked before we became aware of the threat of cancer, emphysema, and bronchial disease. Only long-time investigation will determine long-term effect.

Marijuana poses two basic problems. It *will* impair performance, and it's illegal currently. Anything that's illegal is bound to cause trouble to anyone becoming involved. There is also the concern that marijuana use might lead to other drugs. On the other hand, there is such a condition as an "addictive personality" and perhaps that person would get to hard drugs, such as speed or heroin, even if he never saw or heard of marijuana.

In conclusion, it is felt that no drugs in this chapter have any place in the high school athletic picture with the exception of vitamins, aspirin, and the steroids—the cortisones and Butazolidin.

23
Since they pay the bills...

Parental involvement

The cost of this book, either directly or indirectly, will be absorbed by some parent who will be only too glad if the modest investment helps a son or daughter become a better young athlete. Even if that was the only reason, it would be nice to pause here and provide a little recognition and pertinent information to them. It's a toss-up on who sweats more once a game starts, a player or his or her properly concerned parents.

Over the years a number of areas of prime concern to parents have developed. They involve nutrition, taking off weight, fatigue, epidemic conditions, and handicapped youths participating. First, however, a personal plea to all parents to become involved if their child is competing. And, rooting in the stands isn't enough. Parents should, and must, take an active interest without getting in the way, making certain that their child and all the rest are playing under the best conditions.

Medical

What are these? Well, for one, medical. A doctor should be present at all contact sports, and winning shouldn't be put above everything else. The sun will come up the next morning no matter who wins or loses.

What is important is that a youngster's health is protected. And here, of primary concern is someone who has been hurt during the game, and the game is still going on. A parent must be certain that if the athlete is sent back into the game it is with the approval of the attending doctor, and not by the coach alone. And, if a boy has been knocked out, if he has "had his bell rung" as they say in pro football, and someone attempts to send him back, you just come out of the stands as fast as you can and yank the young man off the field.

If a doctor approved the move of sending him back into the game under these circumstances, get the board of education to get another doctor. There is absolutely no reason for ever sending a player back into a game after he has been knocked out. He has sustained a concussion and only bad things can happen if a player who already has a concussion is forced into the position of risking further injury. Your answer is a firm "No" to him, the coach, or anyone else who is intent on risking serious injury to him.

Fatigue

Fatigue is another concern for parents, especially as the season wears on. Any athletic endeavor requires training and puts wear and tear on the body. The body must be compensated with adequate rest. Be on guard against a program where a boy tries to balance school work, athletics, and a job at the expense of sleep and rest. With increasing fatigue, not only do we note an appreciable drop in ability due to muscles being unable to generate a maximum effort, but reflexes are slow and injuries tend to increase dramatically. Part of this may be due to overwork and social activities that cut back on the amount of time for sleep.

We also have the problem of a coach who overworks his players on the theory that if a little bit of practice is good, a lot of practice is better, and a great big load of it is wonderful. Young people won't complain; parents must see for themselves or have an instinctive feeling that something is amiss.

Overwork practice is usually accompanied by too much running and too much calisthenics. If this is calculated to make the player "tough," the coach couldn't be more wrong.

Long practices are unnecessary. After 1½ to 2 hours, concentration and ability to learn drop off sharply. Also, the injury level increases as the fatigue level rises.

Certainly one of the most successful coaches over the years has been Penn State's Joe Paterno. He states he never practices more than 1½ hours. Beyond that, Paterno points out that the learning level drops too sharply and practice is no longer fun. It simply becomes too big a thing to absorb fine details.

Parents, coaches, and everything that catches the athlete's attention should emphasize the fact that rest and sleep are the healing factors most important to the body. Preventive maintenance, along with good nutrition, will enable the body to deliver at the maximum of whatever talent it may have.

Nutrition

Good nutrition? Time and again we see teenagers who are suffering from continued weight losses, especially during a heavy football season. Research into what the average teenager needs to maintain his weight during a football season reveals a staggering need of 6,000 calories daily. This is a difficult thing to accomplish because of a teenager's basic poor eating habits.

Most teenagers simply don't eat breakfast. Nor do they eat mid-morning because they are in school. Lunch is whatever happens to be available. There is no mid-afternoon meal because it is directly before practice. Consequently, we still have the bulk of 6,000 calories for the evening meal and the pre-bedtime feeding. There is no possible way to put 6,000 calories into these two feedings.

A growing athlete also has a high protein need, well above the normal range of 60-plus grams a day needed for body growth. The basic building block for muscle and all the other tissues of the body is protein. Large amounts are necessary to grow and to build the muscles through the exercise programs we've outlined. Many families find it difficult to provide so much protein because it is the most expensive of foods.

Parents should try to bring the student into a multi-meal diet program, avoiding potato chips and other empty-calorie snacks. At the risk of sounding like a broken record, parents should emphasize that good nutrition is a tremendous asset to the athlete and poor nutrition will rob him of a good performance—no matter how much talent there is. The tremendous leap in size and speed by athletes of today over those of twenty and more years ago, along with the drop in times, is not only due to the increase in better training methods but to the marked improvement in teenage nutrition.

Losing weight deliberately, to wrestle in a lower class for instance, poses a tough problem for a parent. What is a safe weight? Medical opinion is often at marked variance with that of the boy or his coach. A rule of thumb is that a boy may not lose more than 5 percent of his body weight before wrestling. This condition *must* vary, however, depending on the individual. Take a flabby boy in an upper weight class. He can lose weight a lot easier and safer than a 100-pounder out to shed five pounds to get into a lighter class. Ideally, a boy should wrestle, or compete in other sports, at a weight where not only is he strong but he looks and feels well.

Once the weight has been taken off, care should be exercised so that it isn't piled on again in an orgy of sandwiches and snack-eating. If that happens the athlete has to go through the entire process again four days later. If he eats a low-calorie diet and maintains a weight that doesn't vary more than a pound or two, he'll be able to withstand better the rigors of the sport.

Laxatives, diuretics (water pills), hot rooms, and sweat suits to make weight are completely unacceptable. They leave the athlete exhausted and unable to compete even though he has made the weight. There's no place in any sports for this kind of conditioning.

Epidemics

Earlier we mentioned "epidemics," which is precisely what we mean. An epidemic of mononucleosis can run right through a team, impetigo can hit nine of ten players on the squad, gastroenteritis can "wipe out" a ball club. Even the common cold develops a broad smile as it contemplates a sports team.

Mononucleosis is born of fatigue, lack of resistance in the body (secondary to fatigue), and close contact among the athletes. Improper diet and poor rest also help keep it going. We find the same basic situation ripe for "mono" in colleges at exam time.

Players pass it along via a community water bucket or water dipper. Portable drinking fountains and squeeze bottles help, but often the player, in his haste, sticks the nozzle into his mouth without thinking, then hands the bottle to the next person in line. And, once someone has used a drinking cup, it becomes suspect.

Impetigo is a contagious skin disease, transmitted from person to person by direct contact either with an open lesion or with a substance or object that has come in contact with that lesion.

In wrestling, the skin is subject to burns from the mat, and impetigo is common in the area of the head gear wrestlers wear to protect their ears. The high humidity generated in the area under the chin straps and the tendency of the chin straps to cause a break in the skin provide an ideal setting for the disease. Borrowing head gear doesn't improve the situation. In other team sports it is passed around by borrowing equipment and using common towels—particularly wet ones.

Injury

Health problems parents should concern themselves with shouldn't exclude the basic question, "Should my child compete?" This, of course, is based on the desire to keep him from being injured. The question shouldn't be should he compete but how strongly injuries influence parents' thinking. There is no question there are injuries in the contact sports such as wrestling and football, and some of these injuries could be severe.

What must be balanced is the possibility of injury against the boy's natural desire to compete in these sports—and what it would mean to him if he was kept out. You notice I used the word "natural." The boy who should *not* compete, particularly in contact sports, is the one who is not convinced this is for him, the boy who goes out for football to prove to his father he is a man or to his girlfriend he is as good as the other boys.

This is the boy who is possibly afraid of contact and, consequently, could get hurt. The boy who plays with abandon, who runs into things as hard as he can, is not the boy who suffers the first injury. It's the boy who hesitates, who stops the moment before the collision to avoid it, who gets badly injured. The thing that scares me most on a football field is to see a boy without desire or talent doing this because his father expects him to be an athlete. This boy is a prime candidate for serious injury. A boy should be permitted to travel at his own pace and go as far as his ability can take him.

Disabilities

We come into the area of medical conditions possibly standing in the way of a boy's competing. Over the years, certain conditions and disabilities have kept boys out. We have picked the ones that no longer have any real importance.

Diabetes: A well-regulated diabetic (under adequate treatment and with his diabetes under good control) should have no problems. There are a number of good major-league baseball players in this category. I don't see diabetes as a bar to high school football, even though I don't know of any diabetics in pro football. Once a player is on good nutrition and regulated, the outpouring of sugar for athletics should be no problem to his body. The healing difficulty through circulatory impairment that occurs in older diabetics is not present usually in a younger person.

Epilepsy: For many years epileptics were barred from contact sports. This is no longer the proper approach. The American Medical Association now feels persons with epilepsy on anti-convulsant medication and under control should be allowed to play *all* sports, including those where head contact is highly possible. The maximum output of effort should have no effect on a controlled epileptic.

Asthma: The limiting factor here is whether the patient can get enough air exchange to his muscles in sufficient quantities to perform. I see no reason why an asthmatic shouldn't take medication to open his airways to permit him to perform.

The Olympic ban against this type of medication was completely unfair. The medicine does contain ephedrine which is considered a cardiac stimulant, but the amount of stimulation is not such that it could improve an asthmatic's athletic ability to any degree. It is interesting that recently new preparations have been okayed by the Olympic officials so that the asthmatic athlete is no longer penalized for his disability.

What you are trying to do is to bring the asthmatic from the impaired level of performance back to the normal level of performance enjoyed by everyone else, thereby allowing him to compete on even terms. Many professional athletes are severe asthmatics and have accomplished enormous feats in competition.

Congenital heart disease: What is the functional capacity of the heart? How much work can the heart do? Can it turn out an adequate amount of work without overstraining itself in doing what the athlete wants to do? If the answer to the last question is *yes,* there is no reason that the athlete shouldn't compete. It is unimportant what the defect in the heart really is; what is important is that the heart is capable of performing despite it. Each case must be individually assessed. It's completely unfair to say to a boy he may not compete because he has a heart defect when, in fact, the capacity of his heart to do the required work is just as good as that of the boy with the normal heart who sits alongside.

Amputation or absence of a limb: There was a recent ruling in a midwestern state keeping a boy from football because of an artificial leg. It was wrong. In spite of heavy handicap, this boy learned to compensate to the point where he had made the team and was able to compete evenly with those who had two good legs. That accomplishment was discounted. It was felt that it was unsafe for him to be on the field and the state wouldn't take the responsibility.

This is difficult to understand. If an artificial limb is "injured" it can be repaired in a factory, rather than in a hospital. The idea that it could possibly be used as a "weapon" in unreasonable. It would certainly be padded to prevent injury to others. It is made of the same plastic as shoulder pads, for instance, and there would be less likelihood of injury on contact than from a ramming helmet.

A boy with this amount of drive shouldn't be penalized. Fifteen years ago we had a boy who had a leg withered by polio. The team not only wanted him but the psychological aspect was such that it was imperative he be allowed to play. Naturally, he couldn't run but he made all-league center and later he said this was the single most important thing in his rehabilitation and his return to a normal way of living.

Handling a handicapped player in sports requires a complete examination of the circumstances. There are physical problems, certainly, but what are the psychological needs? Getting a boy to compete with his peers can change his entire life. That is a tremendous factor which we have often neglected.

Index

A

Abdominal muscle exercises, 45-47, *illus.* 46-47
Achilles tendon exercise, 74
Achilles tendon injuries, 13
Agility development exercises, 74
Alcohol, 88
Amphetamines, 87-88
Amputation or absence of a limb and sports participation, 94
Anabolic steroids, 86
Ankle injuries, 9
Ankle sprain
　anterior, 9
　exercises to prevent, 9-11, *illus.* 10-11
Arch-strengthening exercise, 6
Aspirin, 87
Asthma and sports participation, 94
Astroturf and other artificial turfs, 7

B

Back injuries, 38
Back of the leg exercises, 17, *illus.* 16-17
Back of the leg injuries, 17
Back of the thigh injuries, 25
Back-strengthening exercises, 38-42, *illus.* 38-42
"Burns" from artificial turf, 8
Butazolidin, 86

C

Carew, Rod, vii
Chest-strengthening exercises, 49, *illus.* 49
Children's leagues, 68-69
Cocaine, 88-89
Concentration development, 77
Conditioning, kinds of, 1
Congenital heart disease and sports participation, 94
Coordination development, 68
Cortisone, 86

D

Dedication development, 77
Deep knee bend or "duck waddle" knee injuries, vii-viii, 20
Depressants, 88
Diabetes and sports participation, 94
Diet, 71-72, 81, 92

97

Disabilities and sports participation, 94-95
Dislocation of the shoulder, 51
"Drive-train" injuries related to artificial turf, 8

E

Endurance training, 75
Epidemics among team members, 93
Epilepsy and sports participation, 94
Erving, Julius, vii
Evert, Chris, vii

F

Falling without injury, 74
Foot injury prevention, 5-6
Front of the leg injuries, 15
Front of the thigh injuries, 25

G

Gaining weight, 72
Game rules, knowledge of, 78
Gatorade, 76
Gluteal injuries, 35
Gluteal muscle exercises, 35
Groin-strengthening exercises, 32-35, *illus.* 32-35

H

Hamstring pull, 2
Head injuries, 65-66
Headgear and injury prevention, 65
Heart disease and sports participation, 94
Hernia prevention, 45
Heroin, 88-89
High-heeled shoes, affect of on the Achilles tendon, 14
Hyperextension of the neck, 61
Hyperflexion of the neck, 61

I

Ideal isotonic exercises, 2
Injuries related to artificial turf, 7-8
Isokinetic
   definition of, 2
   machines, 2
Isometric, definition of, 1
Isotonic, definition of, 1-2

J-K

Jackson, Reggie, vii
Knee, importance and vulnerability of, 19-20

Knee injuries, 19-20
Knee-strengthening exercises, 20-24, *illus.* 21-23

L

Lateral ankle sprain, 9
Lateral hyperflexion of the neck, 61
Leg muscle build-up, 80-81
Levy, Dr. Allan, vii
Losing weight, 72, 93
Low-back instability, 37-38

M

Marijuana, 89
Maturity development, 77
Medial ankle sprain, 9
Mental conditioning, 68-69
Mini-Gym, 83-84
Muscle pull, 2
Muscle tear, 2

N

Nautilus, 83-84
Neck braces, 62
Neck injuries, 61-63
Neck-strengthening exercises, 63, *illus.* 62-63
Nicklaus, Jack, vii
Nutrition, 71-72, 81, 92

O-P

Orthotron, 83-84
Parental attitude toward injury, 93-94
Parental involvement in children's sports, 91-95
Paterno, Joe, 92
Payton, Watt, vii
Physical conditioning, 67-68
Potassium level maintenance, 76
Practice length, 92

R-S

Recovery of balance drills, 74
Running, 73, 75, 80
Salt replacement, 75-76
Seaver, Tom, vii
"Shin splints," cause and preventive treatment of, 15
Shoulder injuries, 51-53
Shoulder separations related to artificial turf, 8
Shoulder-strengthening exercises, 55-56, *illus.* 52-57
Sleep, 71

Speed development, 68
"Spearing" and neck injuries, 63
Sportade, 76
Sprinting, 73-74
Stamina development, 68
Standard endurance program chart, 76
Staubach, Roger, vii
Steroids, 86-87
Stretching and flexing program, theory of, viii
Subluxation of the shoulder, 51
Swimming, 75

T

Tendinitis of the shoulder, 53
Thigh injuries, 25
Thigh-strengthening, 25-30, *illus.* 26-31

U

Understanding, development of, 78
Universal Gym, 2
Unnatural movements in sports, 67-68

V-W

Vitamins, 71-72, 85-86
"Walking off" a sprain, 2
Water intake during play, 76
Webb, Allan, vii-viii
Weight lifting, 79-84
Weight lifting exercises, 81-83
Weight lifting machines, 83-84
Weight training and diet, 81
Weight training equipment, 81
Wrist-strengthening exercises, 59